FURNITECTURE

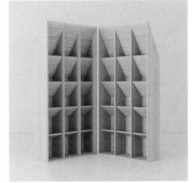  

FURNITECTURE

FURNITURE THAT TRANSFORMS SPACE

ANNA YUDINA

Thames & Hudson

CONTENTS 1

2

3

FURNITURE AS MICRO-ARCHITECTURE   108

SYNTHESIS   194

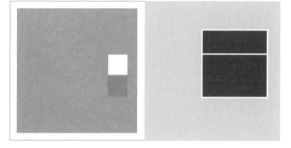

INTRODUCTION

When Le Corbusier introduced his Dom-ino House in 1914, it was a full-speed ahead moment for architects, set free from then on to experiment with façades and floor plans. It was also a seminal moment for furniture designers, as the house's revolutionary slab-and-column construction proved to be the ultimate bookcase.

Odd as it may seem, the essential purpose of architecture and furniture boils down to the same thing: to support, contain and render accessible the third – vertical – dimension of space. In the twentieth century, when the building framework was extracted and highlighted as a subject of technical, functional and aesthetic research, the relationship between architecture and furniture became particularly close.

There is now significant overlap between the two, as they merge into a new class of 'architectural furniture', or split into modules that can serve as building blocks for both pieces of furniture and works of architecture. This brings us to two complementary lines of research that have different starting points, but share the common aim of creating maximum impact from minimum resources, whether space, time or materials.

Focused on the potentials of the structural framework, the architecture-to-furniture line of enquiry is about flexibility, transparency and developing structural principles that allow for as many different 'user scenarios' as possible – capable, like the Dom-ino system, of supporting virtually any kind of design programme and interior layout.

The opposite vector of furniture-to-architecture deals with 'compacting the content', producing furniture that morphs into micro-architecture and blurs the boundary between an XL furniture piece and an XS building – think of Verner Panton's Visiona 2 (1970), Joe Colombo's Total Furnishing Unit (1971), and a whole array of pioneering 'mobile-environment' designs developed for the exhibition 'Italy: The New Domestic Landscape' held at the Museum of Modern Art in 1972.

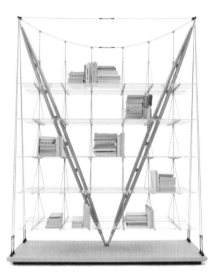

ARCHITECTURE TO FURNITURE (CLOCKWISE, FROM TOP LEFT):

VELIERO, FRANCO ALBINI, 1940 (CASSINA I MAESTRI COLLECTION)
EAMES STORAGE UNITS, CHARLES AND RAY EAMES, 1949 (VITRA)
INFINITO, FRANCO ALBINI, 1956–7 (CASSINA I MAESTRI COLLECTION)
NUAGE, CHARLOTTE PERRIAND, 1952–6 (CASSINA I MAESTRI COLLECTION)

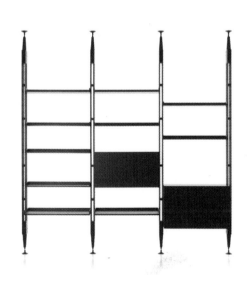

Colombo's Kitchen, Bathroom, Cupboard, and Bed and Privacy cells, with their built-in, fold-out furniture, could function as autonomous rooms-within-a-room, or be combined to form the Total Furnishing Unit (28 m^2, or 301 sq ft), a fully equipped 'futuristic habitat'. Ettore Sottsass's design for a portable, flexible home served a similar purpose, but maximized the modular quality. Assembled from uniformly shaped rectangular plug-ins, it allowed users to rearrange different functions as if they were parts of a DIY kit.

Richard Sapper and Marco Zanuso's Mobile Housing Unit, also exhibited in 1972, brought together architecture, furniture, mobility and industrial standardization to explore yet another problematic. They used an ISO container to produce an emergency shelter that could be adapted to any means of commercial transportation, ready for immediate deployment. One of the project's main features was its side wall, which folded down to form a terrace, doubling the usable space.

Both 'structural' and 'integrative' paths bring about new ways of interacting with the space we inhabit. The website accompanying the exhibition 'Atelier à habiter' (2013–14), curated by Evelien Bracke and held at contemporary art centre Z33 in Hasselt, Belgium, sums it up neatly: 'All over the world we are confronted by new demographic, social, environmental and economic challenges and the reinvention of systems. Likewise, architecture and «dwelling» are also being reinvented. Will the modernistic *machine à habiter*, built from standard elements for standard needs, shift into the *atelier à habiter*, where the creative resident stands out as a planner, organizer and designer?'

The more than two hundred architecture/furniture crossovers brought together in this book are certainly not exhaustive. When scrolling through the countless possibilities that appear on the border between the two domains, we are only just tapping into the extreme and fascinating diversity of … furnitecture.

FURNITURE TO ARCHITECTURE: PHANTASY LANDSCAPE, VISIONA 2, VERNER PANTON, 1970 [P. 10]

FURNITURE TO ARCHITECTURE: TOTAL FURNISHING UNIT, JOE COLOMBO, 1971

1

EXPERIMENTING WITH STRUCTURE

A zoom-in into the architectural logic of furniture design inevitably takes us to the starting point: the structural frame and the variety of experimental work it can inspire. Designers x-ray through outer layers, resolving a piece of furniture into irreducible elements: the shelf (= a slab, horizontal, support for the contents) and the upright (= a column, vertical, support for the support). The framework is looked at from a triple perspective: technical, functional and expressive.

The challenge is to maintain structural stability while mini-mizing the amount of materials, and expand the functional limits, before seeing how all of this creates new formal beauty. Thus, Martin Szekely (p. 23) wants his designs to be so minimal and understated they might be regarded as commonplace; Peter Marigold (pp. 42, 62) visualizes geo-metrical laws through shelving that resembles cellular structures; KiBiSi (p. 28) swap verticals and horizontals; Lith Lith Lundin (p. 50) adapt the principles of tensegrity to locally sourced wood and leather; and Massimo Mariani (p. 102) draws upon mathematical models to design a storage wall that enables virtually infinite combinations, all of which are both functional and aesthetically valid.

This first chapter focuses almost exclusively on furni-ture, highlighting the different facets of structure-based experiments. In the section 'Frameworks', designers inves-tigate the functional essence of the structure, while in 'Deconstruction' they take the structure to pieces and look into the meaning of each part. They examine the forces that keep these parts together, and creatively reassemble them to change the way we interact with our furniture and feel about the spaces we inhabit. They explore the relationships between art and design, the rational and the intuitive.

'Blocks & Modules' is about obtaining maximum variety with only a few basic elements and smart, often tools-free solutions to assemble them. In 'Stacks & Towers', furniture design finds direct inspiration in urban landscapes, and, like architecture, benefits from space-saving vertical construction to combine high density with flexibility. In 'Transformers', designers explore the capacities of movement as the fourth dimension: a cube unfolds into a complex sculpture comprised of drawers; a pillar integrates rotating shelves and racks for a constantly changing interior.

Closing the sequence of experimental frameworks is 'Parametrics', a few examples of more sophisticated customization where the final shape of a piece of furniture is defined by both the user and the space for which it has been designed. Advanced software manipulates and synchronizes several parameters at a time, morphing basic modules into bookcases, or storage walls, or interior landscapes that fill the entire room, ceilings included, and incorporate light fixtures, service windows, and so on.

Further along, we are going to see more of modular and parametric design, this time applied to large-scale building blocks where furniture is just one of multiple integrated functions. There will also be more of transformers, hybrids and furnitectural landscapes.

FRAMEWORKS

FRAMEWORKS, STUDIO MIEKE MEIJER (P. 27)

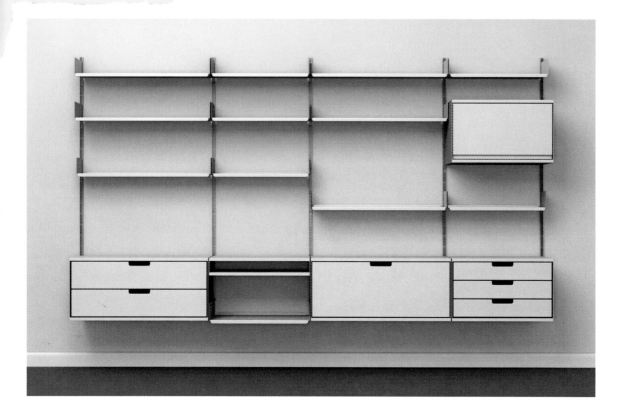

606 UNIVERSAL SHELVING SYSTEM
DIETER RAMS / VITSOE.COM

Dieter Rams is the name behind some of the twentieth century's breakthrough product designs. The 606 Universal Shelving System stems from his long career at Braun, where his first job in the 1950s was to modernize the company's interiors. Among Rams's early efforts were initial ideas for a track-based storage system, the aim of which was to achieve easy assembly and maximum variability from the minimum number of industrially manufactured parts. Launched in 1960 by furniture manufacturer Vitsœ, it has been in production ever since. The system comprises aluminium 'E-Tracks' and 'X-Posts', to which interchangeable shelves, cabinets and tables can be mounted, using no tools. This allows for further additions and updates: at Vitsœ, more than half of the orders come from existing customers.

HEROIC SHELVES,
HEROIC CARBON DESK
MARTIN SZEKELY / GALERIEKREO.FR

Martin Szekely's Heroic Shelves
(bottom left), from 2009 and produced
in a limited edition by Galerie Kreo,
are about reducing the structure to its
bare minimum. All that remains are thin
aluminium composite panels, reinforced
at the intersections with cross-shaped
profiles. With Heroic Carbon Desk
(left), from 2010, Szekely carries his
project still further. The simplicity of the
desk belies its complex technology:
a cross-section reveals several layers
of materials, including aluminium
honeycomb and sheeting, resin and
glue. This sandwiching of materials and
the resulting thickness were calculated
so that the desk will not bend through
normal use. The single-line principle
can be applied across an entire range
of furniture, from seating to shelves.

RANDOM

NEULAND PASTER & GELDMACHER /
MDFITALIA.IT

By shifting the focus from container to content, designers Eva Paster and Michael Geldmacher rethink the traditional method of displaying books on horizontal shelves. Behind their philosophy is the idea that because books are carriers of thoughts and memories, and because thoughts are free, the books themselves should also be granted freedom. Thus, the Random shelving unit (below) is defined by vertical compartments of varied dimensions, allowing for a more personalized organization of libraries. The ultra-slim structure and bright-white colour ensure the books stand out.

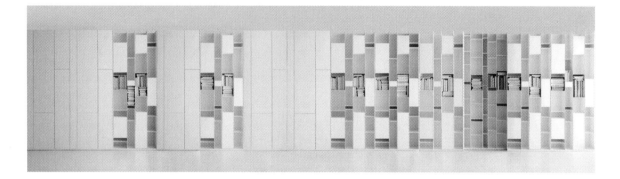

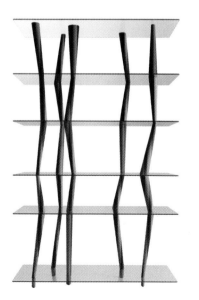

SENDAI

TOYO ITO / HORM.IT

This bookcase (left) reinterprets the design essence of architect Toyo Ito's mediatheque in Sendai, Japan, a transparent building in which six slabs are supported by irregularly shaped steel lattice columns, stretching from the ground plane to the roof.

DISPLAY

ALEX MACDONALD /
EANDY.COM

Alex Macdonald's Display shelves (left) exploit the bending qualities of plywood, which provides the curvilinear form, while at the same time making it possible for the product to be flatpacked.

FLAT.C
ANTONIO CITTERIO / BEBITALIA.COM

To design an up-to-date shelving system, architect and designer Antonio Citterio looked into the evolution of the bookcase typology over the last few decades. Key issues included the addition of home office and entertainment functions, balancing the shrinking presence of books with ever-larger television screens, and fitting video equipment harmoniously into the home environment. The result is Flat.C, the basic element of which is a custom-developed, self-supporting aluminium structure that enables an impressive 3.5 m (11 ft) shelf span and uses a system of hidden yet accessible cable ducts. The structure itself is exceptionally compact, and the varying depths of the shelves create plenty of space for bulky objects. Cantilevered containers, open and closed, provide smart storage and animate the façade.

TIPI
ASSAF ISRAEL / JOYNOUT.COM

Designer Assaf Israel infuses traditionally static objects with a sense of dynamism. Developed for his own label Joynout, the all-wooden Tipi modular shelving system (left and below) serves as a bookcase, desk and open wardrobe. The cone-shaped structure is easy to assemble, requiring only twelve screws, and the circular holes cut into the shelves allow them to be positioned at the desired height without the need for further fixation.

WEAVE
CHICAKO IBARAKI / CASAMANIA.IT

Chicako Ibaraki's design for a freestanding bookcase (above) is shaped from flat, interlocking steel bars, and can hold up to two hundred books. The perpendicular arrangement creates shelving space, and the rubber coating prevents books from slipping.

FRAMEWORKS
STUDIO MIEKE MEIJER

Frameworks, by Mieke Meijer and Roy Letterlé of Dutch design firm Studio Mieke Meijer, originated from experiments with a lattice-based structural system. Thin oak slats connected by steel plates and rivets form an exceptionally stable structure, which can create large spans with the minimum use of materials. Initially interested in using such structures to demarcate spaces, the designers then added glass shelves, upgrading the partition to a lightweight and transparent storage item.

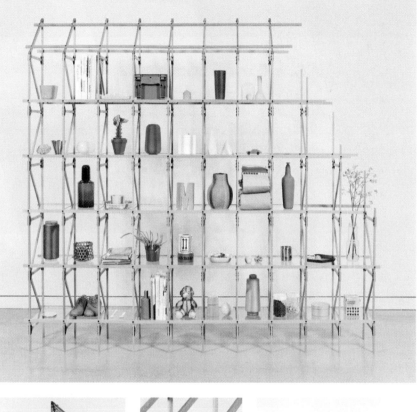

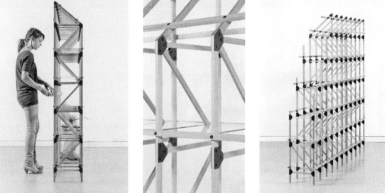

SLICE

KIBISI / ANDTRADITION.COM

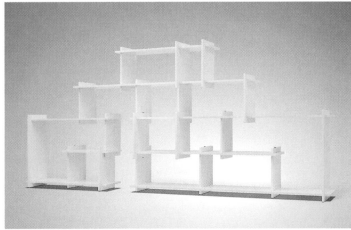

When asked to design a shelving system that would be suitable for contexts from a living room to a retail store, Danish design firm KiBiSi decided to build a regular structure with the potential to go wild. To accommodate a wider array of objects and uses, they took a traditional construction system and rotated it 90°. Shelving usually consists of vertical boards with a dotted line of holes, to which horizontal boards are fixed with the help of pins, with a cross element at the back ensuring structural stability. Here, stability is an inherent quality: holes are drilled into the horizontal boards, and the vertical boards are locked onto them.

YUU

TOTON & CO / YUU.EU.COM

Designed by Paris-based Toton & Co, the slender but robust YUU integrates any architectonic issues effortlessly, from doors and columns to panel radiators and cable ducts. The design, a mere 12 cm (5 in.) deep, can be used in tight places, including hallways and balconies.

The system is based around two components: an aluminium profile and a patented clamping element that secures three rectangular bars together. Add-on accessories adapt it to any indoor and outdoor application, from a library or kitchen to a green wall.

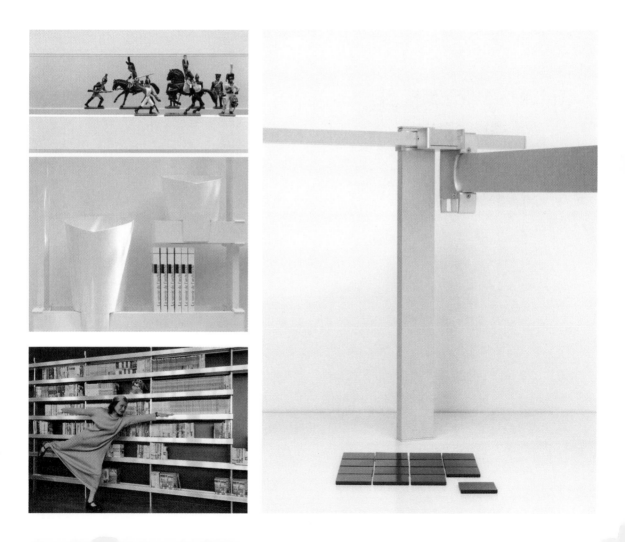

SPIRAL
PHILIPPE NIGRO

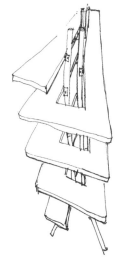

Designer Philippe Nigro's shelving system (left and below) is a plywood spiral deployed around vertical supports, ensuring the structure's rigidity and stability. Metallic fixtures allow for precise positioning of the shelves.

MINIMUMBOOK
GIUSEPPE AMATO / MINIMUMBOOK.COM

Born out of designer Giuseppe Amato's vision of a shipwreck, filled with ancient manuscripts and recovered by archaeologists centuries later, MinimumBook (above and below) juxtaposes powerful verticals and rugged horizontals: steel rods and oak shelves; the poetic imperfection of old wood and the industrial quality of stainless steel. This is a naked structure that doesn't hide a single joint.

PARALLEL
STEPHEN BURKS /
MODUSFURNITURE.CO.UK

This bookcase (above and right) by American designer Stephen Burks is a zigzag arrangement of 'ladders', held together by CNC-contoured shelves. The fine detailing combines aesthetics and function, adding refinement and ensuring that the shelves sit snugly in place.

COMFY CARGO CHAIR
STEPHAN SCHULZ

Stephan Schulz stripped an armchair down to the wireframe, both to minimize the use of materials and to add (or rather insert) some extra functions. Thanks to its hollowed-out skeletal design, the digitally manufactured Comfy Cargo Chair (above) – sixty-six curved components, 52.5 m (172 ft) of steel wire and 50 cm^3 (3 cu. in.) of volumetric capacity, all within an average armchair weight – can be stuffed with anything from books to clothes, not to mention a couple of plant pots and a clip-on reading lamp.

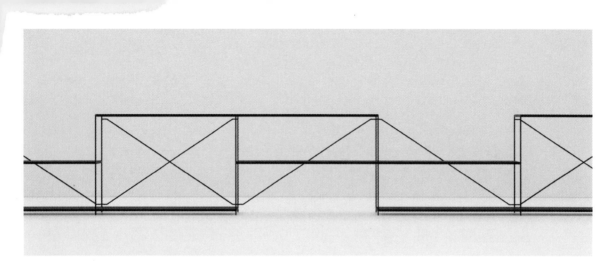

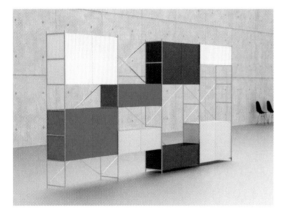

R.I.G.
MIKAL HARRSEN /
MAUSTUDIO.NET

The name R.I.G., standing for Rudimentary Interior Geometry, implies the intention to design 'something as fundamental as possible', as Mikal Harrsen of Danish label MA/U Studio explains. The use of basic construction techniques focuses attention on the structure and materials, as the desks and storage systems are meant to adapt to all kinds of purposes and environments.

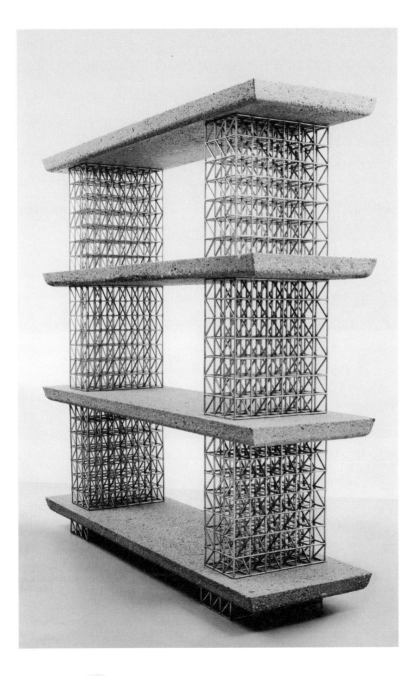

GRIDLOCK
PHILIPPE MALOUIN

For Philippe Malouin's Gridlock series, standard timber slats were multiplied, then rotated around an axis to create the supporting structure. 'The resulting table gives the impression of a building with columns and ceiling,' he explains. The initial form evolves into other functional pieces, including seats, benches and bookshelves, through simple stacking and the addition of horizontal slabs.

Philippe Malouin
New works

DRIZZLE
LUCA NICHETTO / GALLOTTIRADICE.IT

In Italian designer Luca Nichetto's
bookcase (below), the structure is
reduced to just a few hints. Reminiscent
of light rain – as suggested by its
name – Drizzle has thin, asymmetrically
arranged vertical parts that appear to
dissolve in the air before touching the
ground. Technically, the design allows for
a variety of iterations: placing multiple
units next to each other enhances the
rainwall effect, while the modest size of a
single unit is more suited for tight spaces.

USEFUL LIVING
SANGHYEOK LEE

Useful Living (left and below) is a ready-
to-assemble furniture set that mimics
scaffolding. It is also the manifestation
of Korea-born, Berlin-based Sanghyeok
Lee's memories of his nomadic lifestyle
as a young designer. The use of oak and
meticulous detailing are borrowed from
classic Danish furniture; Lee perfected
his design at the Danish Art Workshops,
while staying true to the original concept
of things so basic and unpretentious,
they may pass unnoticed.

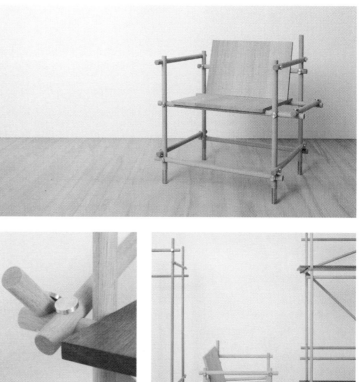

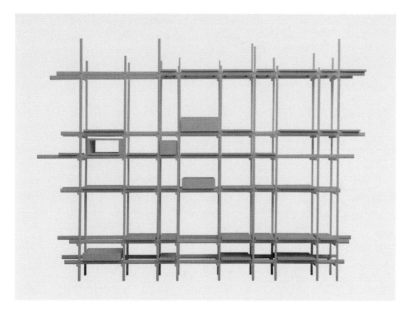

XYZ
LHOAS & LHOAS / MOCALINE.COM

XYZ by Belgian architectural duo Pierre
and Pablo Lhoas is an homage to the
furniture designs of Gerrit Rietveld and
architect Frederick Kiesler's City
of Space. This seemingly simple shelving
unit is in fact a complex assemblage
of polygonal-section wood battens. Their
intersections ensure the rigidity of the
main structure, which, in turn, provides
a grid that allows users to arrange and
rearrange shelves and storage boxes
according to their needs and moods.

ES
KONSTANTIN GRCIC / MOORMANN.DE

Es is German designer Konstantin
Grcic's take on stability – who said
shelves shouldn't wobble? The design
is both tongue-in-cheek and deceptive:
the uprights (if they can be called that)
may be tilted to the right or left, yet
the shelves remain horizontal and are
capable of bearing heavy loads.

METROPOLIS
GIACOMO MOOR / MEMPHIS-MILANO.IT

Created by Giacomo Moor for Post Design Gallery, the
Metropolis collection (below and opposite) consists of seven
pieces of furniture, which, as he says, 'evoke archetypal
metropolis skylines'. A degree of abstraction is achieved by
separating the storage compartments from the supporting
structure. The black metallic framework is occasionally
punctuated by rectangular wooden volumes, with the absence
of visible handles reinforcing their architectural presence.

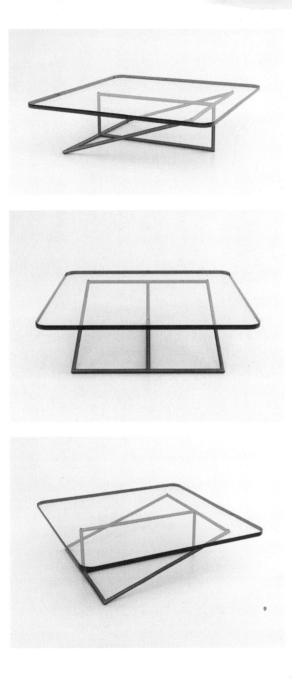

STAN
LUIS ARRIVILLAGA

This transparent tabletop (right) reveals a visually lightweight
and dynamically balanced pedestal. The use of material
in the tubular steel structure is limited to the bare minimum.
Drawing inspiration from Piet Mondrian's geometric paintings,
designer Luis Arrivillaga has manipulated contours and voids
to create a shape that seems to change as the user moves
around the table.

6×6

GRANDE

Aurélie Mathieu and Charlotte Sunnen of Grande joined forces with marble masons Gros-Dérudet to develop a new material that would have the potential to overcome industry constraints. Taking wood laminate as their guide, they glued up a stone sandwich, then cut it into 6×6 cm (2×2 in.) battens, significantly enhancing the material's rigidity. Apart from the increased production quantities, the project offers solutions for utilizing industry remnants. This design is a piece of display furniture that highlights the new aesthetics of laminated stone, and hints at larger structures that can be built using the same method.

EN YU-AN

TOKYO, JAPAN
FUMIHIKO SANO

Japanese company Maruwakaya specializes in *monozukuri*, which can be loosely translated as the 'art of making things'; its Tokyo gallery showcases one-of-a-kind pieces that link traditional crafts and contemporary art. Architect Fumihiko Sano filled the gallery space with a minimalist installation – a wooden structure composed of lintels and pillars – which provides both functionality and atmosphere. Independent from the walls, floor and ceiling, this space-making piece of furniture subdivides the room and integrates the counter and display shelves.

DECONSTRUCTION

SPLIT, SUM, TILT
PETER MARIGOLD / SCP.CO.UK

Split (left) is based on the simple geometric principle that the inverted angles of a split form will always total 360°. 'When arranged into larger structures, the boxes become reminiscent of other cellular structures,' notes designer Peter Marigold. 'Skin cells, perhaps, or aerial views of fields from the sky.' Sum (far left, bottom) is a production interpretation of the principle, issued by British manufacturer SCP. This wall-mounted asymmetrical shelving system uses three modular shapes, designed to fit together in an infinite number of ways. Tilt (above and top left) adapts the 360° principle further to include freestanding units.

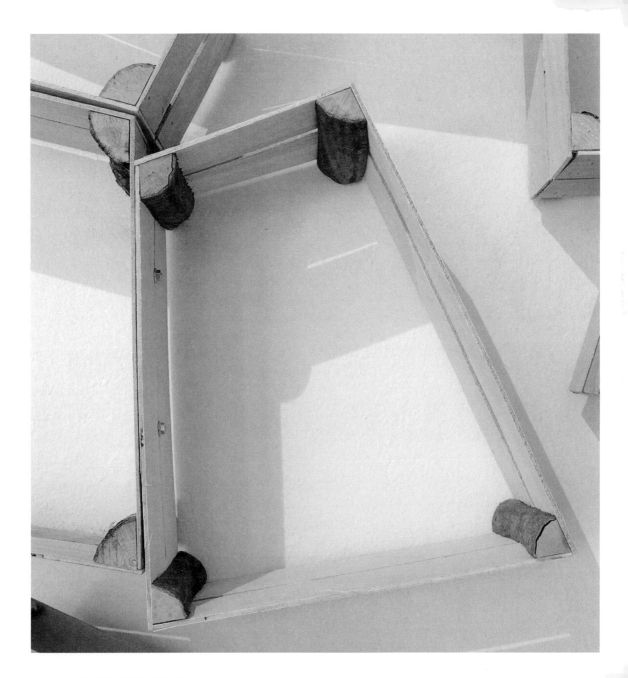

SLAGBAENK, WEEDS, JASON
RASMUS B. FEX

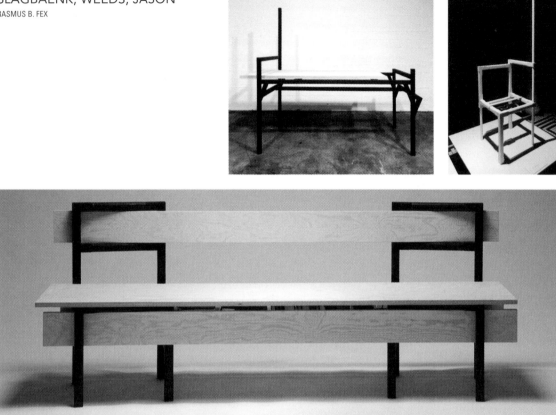

By exploring the borderland between conceptual and functional, Danish designer Rasmus B. Fex has developed a method that he sums up as 'art with function, design without'. Slagbaenk (above and left) is a deconstruction of the kitchen bench, a typology that is firmly rooted in Scandinavian furniture history. Maintaining its triple function (bench, storage and daybed), it consists of two chairs connected by five wooden planks, the lengths of which are determined by the desired dimensions of the bench. Weeds (top left) and Jason (top right) are two further examples of the cross-fertilization between art and design.

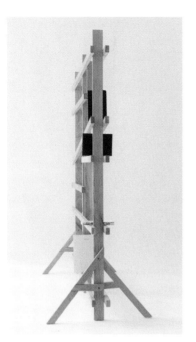

LATTE
ALEX VALDER

German designer Alex Valder's Latte bookcase (left and below) is intended as a DIY item, assembled from standardized pre-drilled wooden slats, using downloadable instructions. The piece's structural stability is ensured by a diagonal slat, which also creates a strong, formal element.

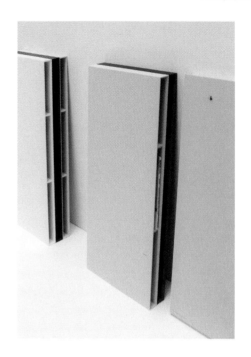

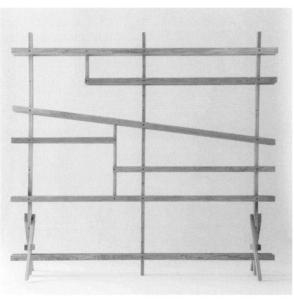

7.5 COLOR SPACE
SEONGYONG LEE

A wooden panel leaning casually against a wall in the street provided the inspiration for 7.5 Color Space (above). Designer Seongyong Lee wanted to recreate its unobtrusiveness and stability in a functional object – the 7.5° leaning angle ensures both. Accessible from the sides, the shelves are intended for tight spaces and allow room for storage of books and magazines. Leaned against or mounted on a wall, they animate a space with their bright colours and clean lines.

TYKE
KONSTANTIN GRCIC /
MAGISDESIGN.COM

Part of The Wild Bunch furniture
series designed by Konstantin
Grcic, Tyke (left) is an exercise in
the smart reduction of structure,
material and effort of assembly.
Its uprights lean against the wall,
while shelves of bent steel are
simply hooked onto them.

ITALIC SHELF
RONEN KADUSHIN

Each piece of Open Design,
an accessible product line established
in 2004 by Ronen Kadushin, can be
downloaded as a CAD file, fed to
a CNC machine, then assembled from
the resulting elements in plywood
or metal. The project required some
serious deconstruction thinking from
its designer, who reduced an initial
idea to its basic components, enabling
it to be produced from a single sheet
of material for tools-free assembly.
Italic Shelf (right) uses two modules,
a shelf and spacer, to form all sorts of
configurations, from shelving to micro-
architecture. The principle of 'controlled
collapse' enables structural stability:
each part is held in place by its own
position and weight.

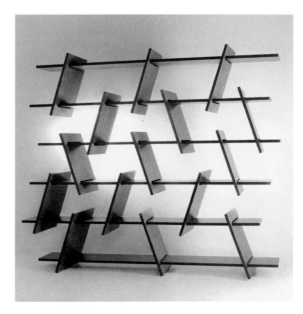

UP SIDE DOWN
DIFFERENT & DIFFERENT

The Up Side Down shelving system (right) by French design collective Different & Different uses thin sheets of steel to form a structure that oscillates between two and three dimensions. The piece can stand on any of its four sides, adapting to each individual space, and to each user's different storage and display needs.

MY OWN PUBLIC ROOM
DITTE HAMMERSTRØM

This project by industrial designer Ditte Hammerstrøm is a new furniture type aimed at making the changing rooms in Denmark's aging public sports facilities more attractive and user-friendly. A series of minimalist racks, each adapted for a particular function, are arranged in groups within a vast changing room to create suitable setups for various types of users, 'from a handball team to a little ballerina'.

WASSERREGAL
NICOLE WERMERS

Artist Nicole Wermers's 'water shelf' (below) inverts
standard industrial shelves to reveal their folded-up edges,
transforming them into a tray for containing water.
The irregular arrangement of U-shaped supports adds
a sense of fragility and weightlessness.

PERSPECTIVE SHELF
OIL MONKEY

For this project (opposite), made from
oak, Hong Kong-based designer and
artist Fuquan Junze of Oil Monkey
applied the principles of perspective
drawing to a physical structure.

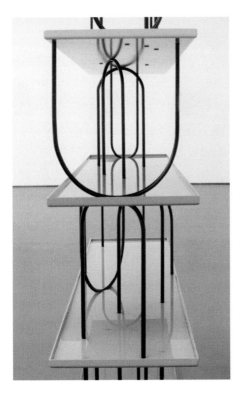

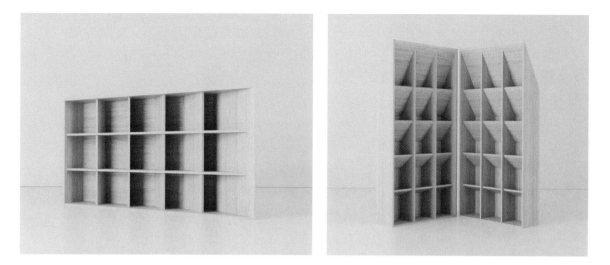

GLIMM, SEVEN
LITH LITH LUNDIN

Delivered as easy-to-assemble kits, Glimm (top left) and Seven (right) stools belong to the Tensegrity family from Swedish designers Lith Lith Lundin. Tensegrity, a structural principle in which components are held together by a combination of tensile and compressive forces, is here applied to leather straps and wooden sticks. The inspiration for the design stems from the way this technique takes full advantage of the qualities of the materials used.

60 SERIES
XYZ INTEGRATED ARCHITECTURE

The tables and chairs from Georgian collective XYZ Integrated Architecture's 60 series are all produced with traditional techniques and materials. They share another trait, as well: their supports are uniformly tilted at 60°. Although the pieces are perfectly stable and operational, the designers note: 'We are tricked into believing that these artefacts teeter on the brink of possibility, and that the force of gravity will soon make them collapse and fall apart.'

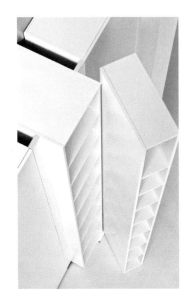

BLIO
NEULAND PASTER & GELDMACHER /
KRISTALIA.IT

By deconstructing and rotating a regular
bookcase, reconfiguring it into a series
of smaller units with side access, Eva
Paster and Michael Geldmacher aimed
to recreate the experience of exploring
a large library, aisle by aisle. 'The act
of entering a bookshelf, instead of just
standing in front of it, intensifies the
immersion into the world of books,'
they explain. A Blio-equipped living
room offers two scenarios: a serene
arrangement of white surfaces, or an
invitation to engage with its secret
compartments.

ETAGÈRE DE COIN
STUDIO DESSUANT BONE / CINNA.FR

This 'corner shelf' by Marie Dessuant
of Studio Dessuant Bone is part of
the Objets Vagues collection, for
which the designer moved away from
straightforward typologies to explore
'areas of hesitation and in-between
spaces', encouraging users to interpret
objects in their own way. This cabinet
of curiosities, leaning against the corner
of a room and perched on a step ladder,
both exploits the unused space and
highlights its emptiness.

MONTIGNY
RODERICK VOS

'The constructivist approach to product
design has always appealed to me as
a designer,' admits Roderick Vos.
This design for a cupboard both borrows
from the Constructivists and argues
with them. A systematic approach
is applied to the structural frame, while
the arrangement of the storage units
appears to be random.

BLOCKS & MODULES

ALDA, GIULIO IACCHETTI (P. 64)

OBU: ORIGINAL BIPOLAR UNITS
BONA-LEMERCIER

Paris-based architects Bona-Lemercier developed the Original Bipolar Units, or OBU, as a multifunctional solution for CNEAI, the national centre for contemporary graphic arts. OBUs form part of an intelligent intervention within a heritage building, and are used as archive storage, exhibition displays, shop equipment, office furniture and video-viewing platforms. Each unit is made up of two steel sheets, bent at 90° and slotted into each other to form a box. Conceived both as modular storage units and building blocks, they are held together by magnetic rubber bands, allowing for complex cantilevered shapes. Easy to build and disassemble, OBUs can repurpose a space in a minimum amount of time.

MAGNETIQUE
SWEN KRAUSE / MOORMANN.DE

The design of Swen
Krause's wall-mounted
metal sheet and storage
boxes with magnetic
backs (above) is flexible
enough to allow for
an endless variety
of arrangements and
configurations.

CROSS UNIT
PHILIPPE NIGRO /
GRUPPO-SINTESI.COM

Philippe Nigro created his
partition bookcase (right)
by multiplying a single,
stainless-steel module.
The interlocking modules
form compartments of
differing sizes to contain
CDs, books, magazines,
and so on.

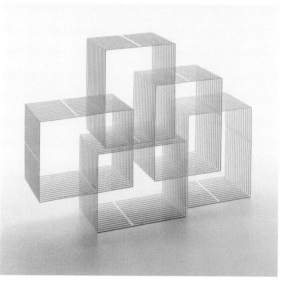

TWIST & LOCK
HARRY THALER

Designer Harry Thaler's
anarchic concept for
a shelving system (left
and below) plays
with traditional apple
crates, which are kept
together by custom-
designed twisting and
locking elements.

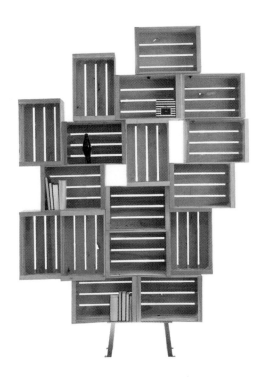

IRKEL
LLOYD SCHWAN / CAPPELLINI.IT

In this design for a bookcase (above),
Lloyd Schwan arranged twelve cylinders
with square compartments inside
them in an orderly formation, resulting
in a boldly graphic statement piece.
'Lloyd wanted to design the way
a child would draw,' explains designer
Constantin Boym, 'without any inhibitions,
with little or no self-control, with creative
freedom unburdened by any kind
of cultural baggage.'

HORIZONTALS

SHIGERU UCHIDA / PASTOE.COM

The Horizontals family of shelves consists not of modules, but of individual objects, and appear like artworks hanging on the wall. Designed by Shigeru Uchida, these long, wood cases have metal doors that slide open to reveal their contents, and are attached by means of an invisible support.

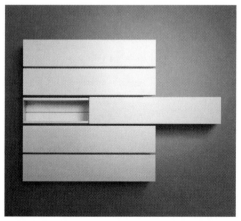

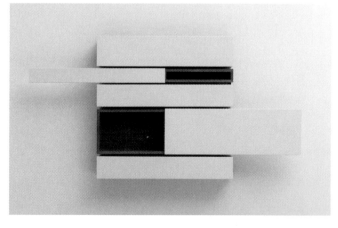

VISION
PIERRE MAZAIRAC, KAREL BOONZAAIJER /
PASTOE.COM

Originally known as the Kubus system when it was launched
in 1965, Vision, designed by Pierre Mazairac and Karel
Boonzaaijer, has been evolving ever since. Conceptually,
the individual pieces were meant as architectural items for
interiors; technically, the invention of new materials (such as
MDF) and new mechanisms (including an invisible snap instead
of a handgrip, or a hinge for manipulating the doors in six
directions) brings the modular boxes ever-closer to the ideal
of formal and functional perfection.

PLAY,
MAKE/SHIFT,
BUILD

ANTOINE PHELOUZAT, PETER MARIGOLD,
JACK GODFREY WOOD, TOM BALLHATCHET /
MOVISI.COM

Stuttgart-based firm Movisi, specialists
in lightweight, tools-free modular
solutions for furniture, teamed up with
Antoine Phelouzat, Peter Marigold, Jack
Godfrey Wood and Tom Ballhatchet to
produce three storage systems with
different functional nuances. Phelouzat's
design for partition shelving, Play (left),
uses three basic elements that are
assembled into rectangular or free-form
configurations. Marigold's self-adjusting
Make/Shift shelves (opposite left, top
and bottom) would fill even the most
awkward of gaps. The corrugated edges
of the wedge-shaped units interlock
to fill niches or odd-shaped spaces.
Finally, Build (opposite right, top to
bottom) by Wood and Ballhatchet is
based on a single, modular element.
An optional backside insert transforms
individual units into transportation boxes,
occasional stools or low tables.

NAN-15
NITZAN COHEN

For NAN-15 (right and below), German designer Nitzan Cohen used modularity to minimize the number of different components needed for a bookcase, and concluded: Why not design the entire structure out of bookends? Taking folded sheet steel as the most common bookend form, Cohen only had to resolve some gravity issues – hence the slanted arrangement of the parts. Based on two modules assembled without tools, the design allows further extension and can act as a room divider (particular attention was given to the view from the back).

ALDA
GIULIO IACCHETTI /
MERITALIA.IT

This partition shelving system by Italian designer Giulio Iacchetti (opposite, top row) minimizes effort of assembly through its three basic elements, which can be mounted onto each other with virtually no limits for height and width.

KOOB
GIULIO IACCHETTI /
ARTHEMAGROUP.IT

Aimed at homes, small offices and retail stores, Koob (opposite, bottom row), also designed by Giulio Iacchetti, uses two modular parts in gracefully shaped sheet steel. Their slightly rounded edges define the system's visual identity.

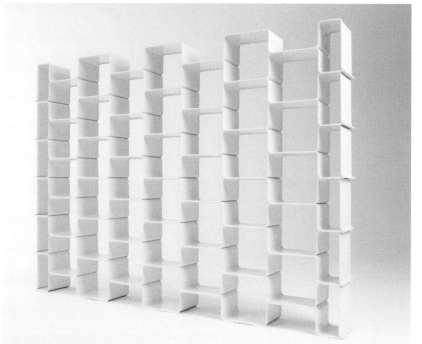

R.A.C.
MIKAL HARRSEN / MAUSTUDIO.NET

R.A.C. (below), another design by Mikal Harrsen for MA/U Studio, is about Randomly Attached Compartments. Intended for tool-free assembly, the storage system uses three elements (a 'tower', a lid/floor module, and a drawer) made from 3 mm ($\frac{1}{10}$ in.)-thick sheet steel. The structure is held together by means of a patented 'lock-disc' mechanism.

C.O.P.
MIKAL HARRSEN / MAUSTUDIO.NET

Designed by Mikal Harrsen for MA/U Studio, Creative Office Project (above) has storage modules that are fixed onto a wall-mounted 'plug and play' railing system, which allows moving and replacing units, and experimenting with multistorey arrangements.

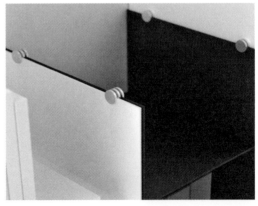

TERRERIA
ARCHEA ASSOCIATI / MOROSO.IT

'Part modular furniture and part Italian farmhouse window', the Terreria concept was originally developed for the interiors of Antinori Winery, in Florence, Italy, and resulted from a long research into poor materials by architectural office Archea Associati. Its terracotta modules are assembled into partition shelving by simple stacking and gluing.

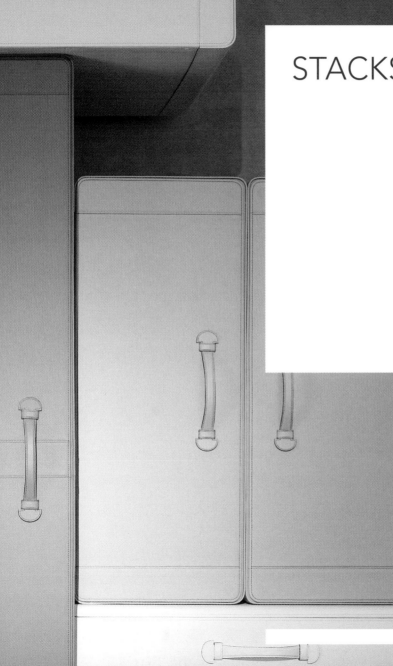

STACKS & TOWERS

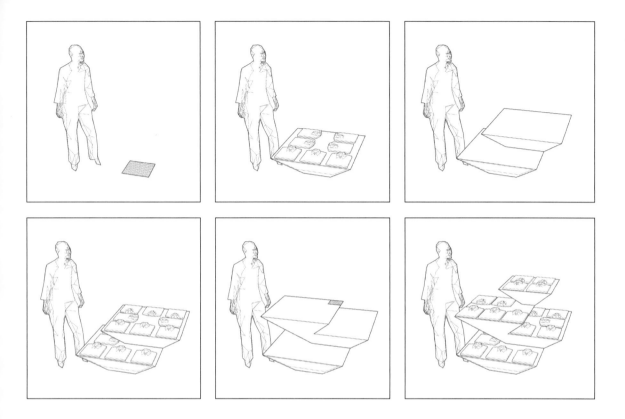

D&V FLAGSHIP STORE

STOCKHOLM, SWEDEN
GUISE ARCHITECTS

Challenged to use every millimetre of space in Swedish clothing
retailers D&V's flagship store, Guise Architects responded
with Top-up, a smart display system with tables that appear to
branch off the main form. Taking a 40 × 40 cm (16 × 16 in.)
patch of floor – as much as one folded shirt would occupy on
a display shelf – the team 'grew' it into an 80 × 80 cm (31 × 31 in.)
table, then repeated the process until the structure reached the
maximum height a customer could conveniently see. By then,
the design provided enough space to lay out some twenty shirts.

INVADER
MARIA BRUUN

A nod to the four-legged AT-AT Walkers in the film *The Empire Strikes Back*, the stackable Invader (below) by Copenhagen-based Maria Bruun wheels around on castors and provides the basic storage options: a drawer, a cabinet and a surface.

TOTEM
VINCENT VAN DUYSEN / PASTOE.COM

Totem (above), a storage tower designed by Belgian architect Vincent Van Duysen, is constructed from square cases and dividing 'turntables', which allow each case to rotate individually.

LONDON
MEIKE HARDE

This design (above) was part of Meike Harde's London series, which rethinks the use of textiles in furniture design. The tower is formed by an elastic fabric that sheaths a metal frame and is tightened at its crossing points, creating see-through compartments for the storage of underwear and accessories.

ROPERO
HIERVE / HFURNITURE.CO

Design firm Hierve, based in Mexico City, cross-bred a wardrobe and a glass cabinet to produce Ropero (left and below left), a series of transparent storage modules, which can be stacked or raised on piles, grouped as a monolith or as separate towers, or lit up to enhance the illusion of a city block in a room.

LAVEER, CALICO
OEUFFICE

These two designs from the Totems for Living series are by Nicolas Bellavance-Lecompte and Jakub Zak of Oeuffice. Sculptural objects 'inspired by the geometries that govern architecture', Laveer (right, top) and Calico (right) are intended to dominate their environment while remaining entirely functional.

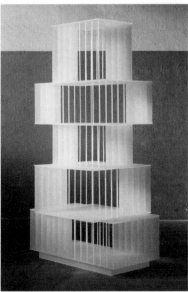

PYRAMID, REVOLVING CABINET
SHIRO KURAMATA / CAPPELLINI.IT

Shiro Kuramata's two architectural takes on the traditional chest of drawers, Pyramid (left), developed in 1968 in transparent acrylic, and Revolving Cabinet (right) from 1970, with its red trays rotating around a vertical metal core, are still in production decades after first being designed. For both projects, Kuramata explored the potential of acrylic, an industrial material that was radically new at the time.

PTOLOMEO
BRUNO RAINALDI / OPINIONCIATTI.COM

The large Ptolomeo family grew from designer Bruno Rainaldi's fascination with piles of books that seemed to defy gravity – an attribute of 'all the houses where books, that indispensable prop of life, are cherished'. Set out to 'translate this fantastic image into a real object', Rainaldi created an invisible bookcase where shelves, reduced to mere props, are hidden between the books.

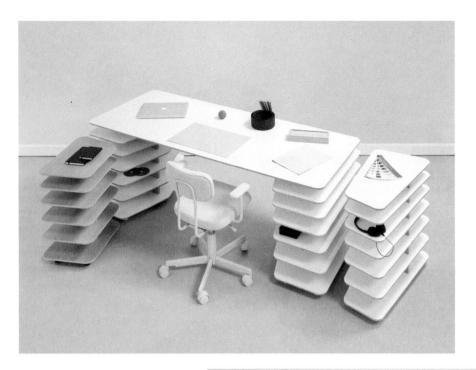

AIR
DANIELE LAGO / LAGO.IT

For the Air series
(opposite, top),
a dematerialized load-
bearing structure with
highly physical horizontal
slabs, designer Daniele
Lago employed
a supporting structure
in transparent glass
to create the illusion of
thick, massive shelves
floating in the air.

STRATES DESK
MATHIEU LEHANNEUR / OBJEKTEN.COM

In creating the Strates Desk (above
and right), French designer Mathieu
Lehanneur drew inspiration from the
layered structure of sedimentary rock.
The easy-to-assemble desk and shelving
hybrid functions both as an individual
unit and as a multi-unit cluster for
shared workspaces.

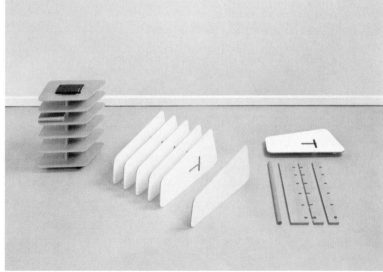

ETAGE
CLAESSON KOIVISTO RUNE / OFFECCT.SE

Swedish architecture and design studio Claesson Koivisto Rune's Etage tables were designed to resemble a model of a building. The set comprises three coffee tables, each composed of three 'slabs', with 40 mm (1½ in.) spacing between them, supported by four 'pillars'. The slabs are orientated in different directions to create spatial tension, which is enhanced by using a different colour for each surface.

MONTANA
PETER J. LASSEN /
MONTANA.DK

Conceived by Danish designer Peter J. Lassen and in
continuous production since 1982, Montana is a 'system design'
that functions like a language: letters add up to words;
words are used to tell personal stories. Here, Lassen created
an alphabet of components for users to design their own rooms.
The shelving range contains forty-two basic units, available
in four depths. The main unit measures 69.6 × 69.6 cm
(27 × 27 in.); the sizes of other units are derived from these
numbers. Together with a set of accessories, they enable more
than a billion combinations.

HYPERNUIT OFFICES

PARIS, FRANCE
H2O ARCHITECTES

When asked to fit out an office for a creative agency, the team at h2o Architectes built a 'landscape' of stacked storage units. The 65 m² (700 sq ft) ground-floor space has a glazed frontage, and hosts five workstations and a meeting room. Prefabricated multi-sized blocks form individual workplaces (defined by the architects as 'living spaces'), partitions and presentation walls. Open towards the rest of the office but enjoying a certain amount of privacy, each work unit can be personalized by reconfiguring the volumes and voids.

SUTOA, DRAWER SHELF
KEIJI ASHIZAWA / FRAMACPH.COM, TANSEISHA.CO.JP

The pyramidal shape of the Sutoa dresser (below and left, top), designed by Keiji Ashizawa, results from its compactness: when taken apart, the drawers nest inside one another; when fully assembled, gaps between the drawers allow them to be opened. Drawer Shelf (left bottom) uses the same kind of rail to both open the drawers and flexibly connect the individual compartments, which glide sideways to expand the available surfaces. In each case, the functional principle becomes elegantly exposed.

LEATHER COLLECTION
MAARTEN DE CEULAER / NILUFAR.COM

This graduation project for the Design Academy Eindhoven was inspired by Belgian designer Maarten De Ceulaer's passion for travelling. A single object soon grew into the Leather Collection, dedicated to 'modern nomads who travel through cities and continents without restrictions or boundaries'. Wardrobes, sideboards and desks hint at a flexible lifestyle, in which luggage and furniture are one and the same thing.

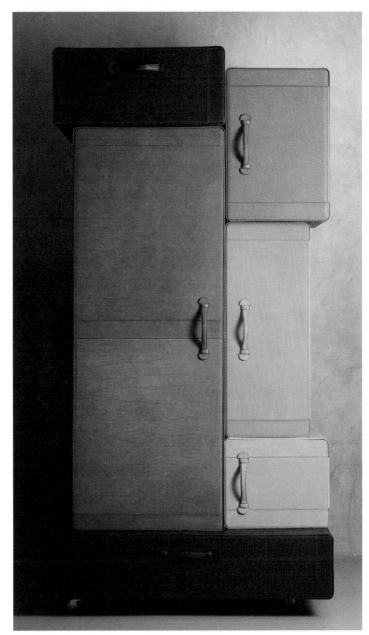

STAIR.CASE
DANNY KUO / OPINIONCIATTI.COM

Taking his cue from the efficiency of high-rise buildings, which maximize density while minimizing the footprint, product designer Danny Kuo applies a similar approach to furniture design. At a height of 2.2 m (7 ft), the top shelves of his vertical cabinet (left and below) would be difficult to reach were it not for the lower drawers, which double up as pull-out stairs.

VERO DRESSER
NADAAA

Useful for storing anything from earrings to linen, the thirty-nine compartments of the Vero Dresser (above) are arranged in layers of decreasing width. In their quest to restrict the design to the bare minimum, the team at NADAAA created a stack of drawers that seems to levitate unaided. 'Even when the corner drawers are opened,' they note, 'no visible backing compromises the structural artifice.' The solution is a scaffold of three aluminium T-sections, aligned with the reveal between the bottom drawers.

STACK
RAW EDGES / ESTABLISHEDANDSONS.COM

Drawers that are left partly open
look more intriguing, believes Shay
Alkalay of London-based Raw Edges,
a collaboration between Alkalay and
Yael Mer. Chests of drawers whose
height is limited by their exterior frames,
and whose drawers only open in one
direction, are boring. The design duo's
Stack, therefore, is a tower of 'floating'
drawers to be pushed and pulled in both
directions, and built up to any height.

F009 MANHATTAN
FOUNDED

'For us, sustainability is not so much in the materials or manufacturing process,' says designer Richard Schipper of Founded, 'but mainly in the product's capacity to survive the nomadic behaviour of its owners.' Together with Dick Hillen, Schipper designed F009 Manhattan, a shelving system that uses a tools-free mechanism and a minimal set of sheet steel parts to create a large diversity of forms. 'The system can be taken apart and rebuilt in another form in a very short period of time,' he adds, 'without screws or glue and without damaging the product.'

I-JOIST
STEVEN BANKEN

For this cabinet by Dutch designer Steven Banken, beams in solid oak serve the function of drawers, rolling lengthwise across a set of brass wheels. The beams have traceable serial numbers: if the clients grow tired of their I-Joists, Banken explains, the manufacturer can buy them back and reuse them as high-quality construction material.

PERFORMA NUF
BEYONDDESIGN /
PERFORMA-NUF.DE

More than a mere stack of storage boxes, Performa Nuf by Beyonddesign is surprisingly dynamic for its solid appearance. The containers glide effortlessly along a pair of smoothly curved grooves, which are key to the design's functionality and aesthetics.

CONTAINER
ALAIN GILLES / CASAMANIA.IT

Furniture designer Alain Gilles explores architectural logic and creates new skylines by splitting storage functions into separate elements, and reconstructing them in a new and unexpected manner. His sideboard (below) is designed, he says, as a 'dialogue between the containers and a landing dock'; different materials and finishes support a variety of uses.

INDUSTRY
BENJAMIN HUBERT / CASAMANIA.IT

British designer Benjamin Hubert notes that his Industry bookshelf (above) was inspired by construction sites, industrial landscapes and contemporary buildings. Here, the design deconstructs the urban landscape, offering 'a microcosmic reflection of the space that surrounds us'. Disparate items made of concrete, metal and timber – materials typically found in our cities – are bound by a thin, white-painted metal frame, reminiscent of scaffolding.

ARTSHOP 10
BASEL, SWITZERLAND
ZMIK

According to the team at spatial-design studio ZMIK, all of the
furniture for the temporary design shop created for the 2010
Art Basel exhibition can be stored on two pallets. The designers
stacked plywood crates, and fastened them with bright-red
strapping to build a terraced, multi-level, conspicuously low-
tech product display. Accessed from the side, the crates were
also used as a convenient storage space for merchandise.

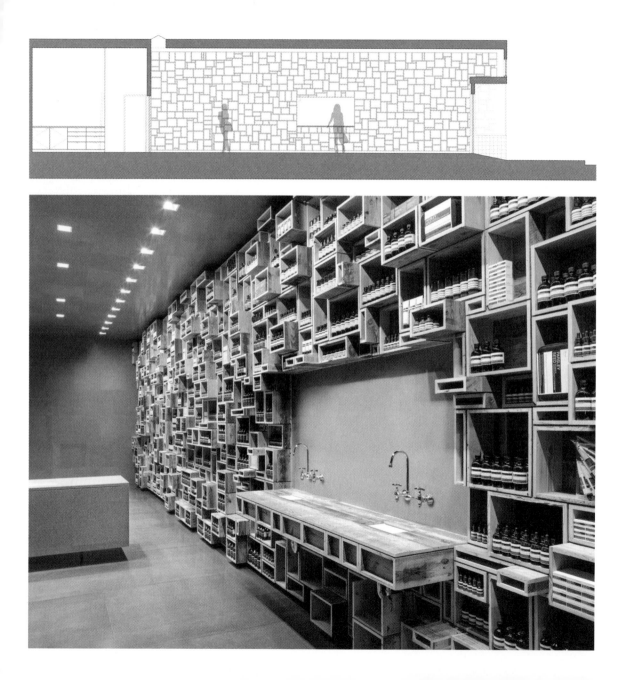

AESOP FILLMORE STREET

SAN FRANCISCO, CALIFORNIA
NADAAA

This shop in San Francisco, California, is located in what architects NADAAA describe as a peculiar space, with a height greater than its width and length several times longer than either. The entire contents are stored in one wall unit, a pixellated 'tapestry' of reclaimed wood boxes that serve as display frames for the different products. The box wall is fashioned from six different modules, defined by product sizes. Modulation made it possible to avoid gaps and overlaps; each individually produced box was mapped to a specific location in the installation. A cork wall, ceiling, counter and bench, together with a masonite floor in a matching colour, counterbalance this high-density display architecture.

TRANSFORMERS

Y'S STORE, RON ARAD ASSOCIATES (P. 99)

FJARILL, IO

JAKOB JØRGENSEN

Jakob Jørgensen is interested in 'joining things', and seeing what happens. 'If you develop a new technique,' he says, 'it is more likely that a new and original design will emerge.' Take Fjarill (left), for example, a chest of drawers that expands into complex, geometrically organic forms as drawers are pulled out. 'Without this flexible joint, which is a purely technical thing,' Jørgensen explains, 'you couldn't have designed an object like that. In the beginning it was just an experiment without any function, but then I realized how it could be used.' Another example, Io (opposite), is a transformer bookcase, with an exceptional variability that is also based around a single, custom-designed joint.

VEGETALE
RANDY FEYS

Belgian designer Randy Feys used a
trunk-like base and series of extensions,
or branches, for his Vegetale collection
(below), which was inspired by plants'
capacity for growth and self-renewal.
Interchangeable 'branches' serve as
coffee tables, shelves and storage units.

JOY
ACHILLE CASTIGLIONI / ZANOTTA.IT

Joy by Achille Castiglioni (left and below)
is a furniture typology based on a spiral
staircase, in which steps rotate around
the pivot and become shelves, complete
with a desk. The design consists of up
to seven L-shaped shelves, which can
flatten into a space-saving configuration,
or unfold into more complex geometries.

THE OUTSIDER / THE INSIDER
BENANDSEBASTIAN

This two-in-one design by Danish duo benandsebastian invites users to contemplate the 'enormous complexity and energy needed to achieve an appearance of simplicity'. Stripped to its bare bones, the Insider (above right) is a slender form cast in white concrete, while the Outsider (top right) is structurally complex and elaborately detailed. Made to be unfolded and opened up, the Outsider reveals the Insider in stages (above left), 'in a form of undressing'.

MOTION

ELISABETH LUX / PASTOE.COM

Berlin-based Elisabeth Lux, an artist with an architectural background, is interested in the transition between 2D and 3D thinking. Her project Motion was born from the idea of connecting two volumes via a shared axis, to add movement and achieve a truly 3D object.

Because the final version had to be hollow, owing to its size, Lux opened up the rectangular elements on one side and made them functional, turning an artwork into a storage system with a custom-developed invisible hinge.

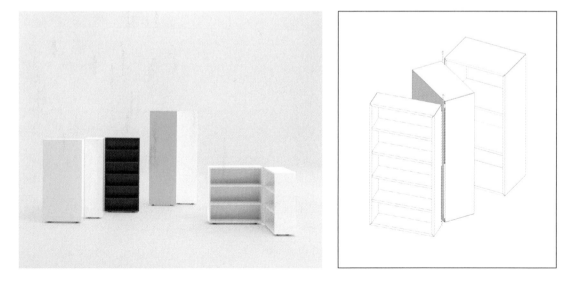

TRANSFORMER SHELF
MARTIN SÄMMER

This project by Martin Sämmer was meant to be an interactive object, whose function would transcend merely practical need: the very process of using it is about constantly redesigning it. When closed, its eight pull-out containers, designed to offer maximum usable space, form a compact rectangular chest. When fully deployed, the piece triples its 1.2 m (4 ft) length.

360° KIOSKS

SINGAPORE
STUDIO SKLIM

In designing six retail kiosks for a narrow pier near Singapore's Water Boathouse, architect Kevin Lim of Studio SKLIM maximized flexibility and minimized the footprint by using a smart, centripetal configuration, grafted onto the pillars of existing canopies. Rooted in the local aesthetic of maximum display surface and personalization, each kiosk has four rotating sections for seating, display, storage and lighting. Goods are stored in shelving units that are swung out like the blades of a Swiss Army knife.

Y'S STORE

TOKYO, JAPAN
RON ARAD ASSOCIATES

Tokyo's space-efficient parking solutions have proven
inspirational for retail design. For fashion designer Yohji
Yamamoto's flagship store for his label Y's, Ron Arad based
his concept around four automotive turntable mechanisms,
embedded in the shop floor. These rotating sculptural masses
continually reconfigure themselves, along with the shopper's
retail experience. Each mega-sculpture is centred around
a structural column comprising thirty-four mobile aluminium
loops, which function as hanging rails or bases for shelves.

PARAMETRICS

SOFTSHELF, E/B OFFICE (P. 104)

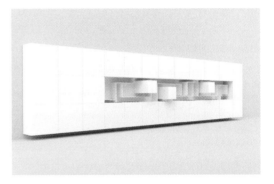

VITA
MASSIMO MARIANI / MDFITALIA.IT

Architect and designer Massimo Mariani uses mathematics and computational design to bring modular furniture to the next evolutionary level. Together with Aedas R&D, he developed interactive software that applies the cellular automaton principle to create functional, consistent and virtually countless configurations of a storage system. Vita is comprised of square modules with shelves and containers, each of which can be rotated 90° in either direction. User-defined parameters (size, module type preference, degree of variability) are fed into an interactive configurator, which responds with possible solutions that can be further adjusted by the client.

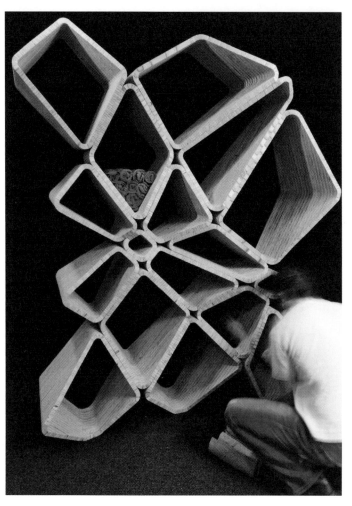

SOFTSHELF
E/B OFFICE

SoftShelf by Yong Ju Lee and Brian Brush of New York-based E/B Office can be personalized by manipulating five customer controls, embedded in a parametric design system: the overall size of the shelf; its curvature; the geometric effect of the shrinking and expanding of boxes; the strength of this effect on the entire piece; and the stretched shape of the boxes. The qualities of the material combined with the precision of CNC milling transform a digital model into a geometrically complex yet sturdy real-life form.

ILLY SHOP

MILAN, ITALY
CATERINA TIAZZOLDI STUDIO

Caterina Tiazzoldi's shelving designs invade the walls and ceiling of Illy Shop, a concept store for the well-known Italian coffee brand. In assessing factors such as product size and number of items on display, Tiazzoldi used parametric software to edit the thickness, opacity, length and explosions of the basic element – a cube, 45 cm (18 in.) per side – to produce two hundred customized units that serve as product displays, a table and counter, casing for light fixtures and video screens, storage boxes and recycling bins.

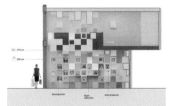

  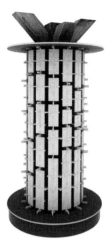 

NOMA LAB

COPENHAGEN, DENMARK
GXN

In designing the Food Lab for one of the world's best-known restaurants, GXN (the innovation unit of Danish architectural firm 3XN) was challenged to develop a storage system that would function as a catalogue of Noma's materials and experiments. The result would be 'a big cell system for displaying ingredients, rather than simply fitting them into traditional kitchen storage'. Since it would be housed in a listed building, the entire system had to be completely independent from the existing structure. The team used parametrics to map the circulation patterns of the staff, light and programme distribution, dimensions of modular units and fabrication requirements. 'It started from very abstract parameters,' they note, 'and ended up at tenths of a millimetre precision, as we had to assemble the units without screws or nails.' To fit in all of the restaurant's utensils and transparent boxes, a total of 5,283 individual parts were created, cut from 249 standard veneer sheets.

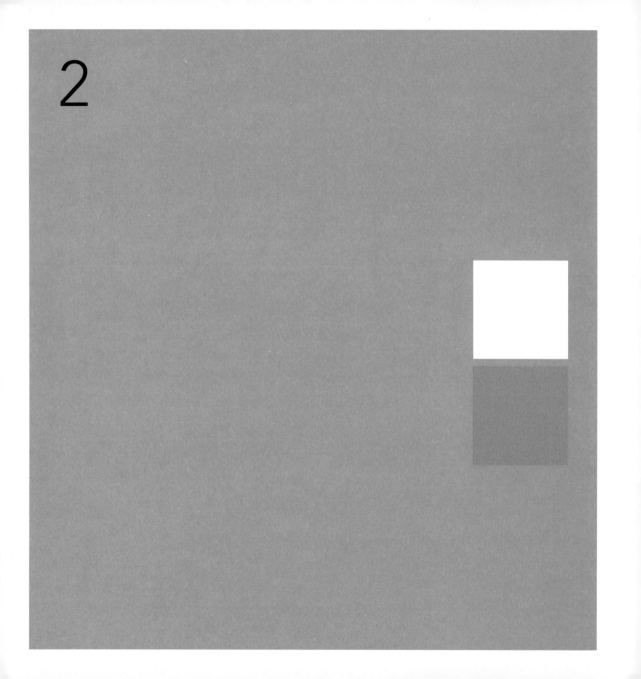

2

FURNITURE AS MICRO-ARCHITECTURE

Like a bookcase, a building can be treated as a generic framework with open-space platforms that are capable of hosting all sorts of contents. This widely practised model can occasionally trigger extraordinary solutions. Aimed at maintaining the flexibility of a space, these designs deliver functionality while leaving plenty of room for future change.

'Architectural furniture', as described by Toshihiko Suzuki of Atelier OPA (pp. 117, 150), is among the solutions. His designs explore the hybrid characteristics of furniture and architecture: they act as room dividers to organize a space; enable necessary functions (storage, workspace, bedroom); and can be folded away. These multipurpose items of furniture can be interpreted as micro-architectural objects, masterplanned across a room.

In this chapter we witness the transformation of furniture into furnitecture, beginning with the section entitled 'Fusion', where separate functions blend into hybrids: playful, practical, artistic and thought-provoking. Here, we again trace two different vectors.

One approach compacts 'architectural furniture' into free-standing items, fixed or mobile ('Space Organizers'; 'Room in a Room'), while the other ('In-built') pulls it in and out of the walls, freeing up the centre of the room for other uses throughout the day. Finally, a series of 'Landscapes' brings us one step closer to the complete merger of furniture and architecture.

FUSION

OBJET ÉLEVÉ, STUDIO MIEKE MEIJER (P. 118)

FURNITURE PROJECT
MULLER VAN SEVEREN

This joint project by Fien Muller and Hannes Van Severen of Belgian firm Muller Van Severen took its inspiration from artist Donald Judd and the Bauhaus. It comprises a chair with a leg extending into a cantilever lamp, an open cabinet with one of the shelves serving as a table and a chaise longue seat integrated into the linear structure, among other designs. By omitting unnecessary details and opting for simplest technological solutions, the designers morph furniture into micro-architectural landscapes. 'As to form or proportion, we do not add anything,' they note. 'The rich marble or vibrant colours of the polyethylene boards create a contrast with the tight form. This piece of furniture battles with minimalism, and uses it at the same time.'

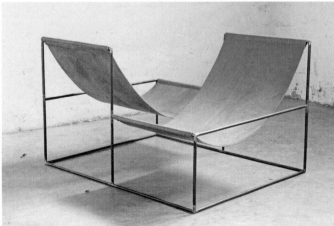

POCKET LANDSCAPE
CIBIC WORKSHOP / DECASTELLI.COM

Impressed by the ways in which nature manifests its force in unexpected contexts – from sprouts finding their way through asphalt to well-tended potted plants that adorn a window sill in a deteriorating neighbourhood – designer Aldo Cibic of Cibic Workshop created a series of Pocket Landscapes (below and right) with iron tabletops that morph into micro-gardens.

WORK AT HOME
STUDIO MAKKINK & BEY / PROOFF.COM

Work At Home is a research cycle initiated by PROOFFLab, the experimental division of furniture manufacturers PROOFF. As part of the experiment, designers from Studio Makkink & Bey dismantled a house and transformed it, fragment by fragment, into mobile work modules that can be plugged into existing buildings. The first in this series of hybrid home-office typologies is a dormer window that has been converted into a compact desk/room-with-a-view (left), which invites the user to work with legs swinging in the air.

PROOFF #006 SIDE SEAT
STUDIO MAKKINK & BEY / PROOFF.COM

Side Seat (below), another design by Studio Makkink & Bey, is intended for 'knowledge landscapes', such as libraries and universities, where work and life merge into one. 'The swivel seat allows users to be interactive and flexible with their workspace, while at the same time creating privacy in public areas,' the designers note. 'Depending on the situation, the table can act as an armrest, a side table or a writing pad.'

A WALL
ATELIER OPA / SHIBASAKI-INC.JP

For this design (above and left), Toshihiko Suzuki of Atelier OPA grafts two environments – work and contemplation – onto one partition screen. The 'on' side is a workspace, complete with a desk, a few shelves and a sofa, 'where brains will work, while the body is relaxed'. The 'off' side offers an armchair with storage space underneath and a side/drink/book table. The entire device, called A Wall, is constructed from aluminium tubes that have been bent to allow seats and supports to 'emerge' from the wall.

OBJET ÉLEVÉ
STUDIO MIEKE MEIJER

A three-part installation for a private residence, Objet Élevé (left), by Mieke Meijer and Roy Letterlé of Studio Mieke Meijer, is more than a staircase: it functions as a connection between two floors, but also provides a workspace and storage. Inspired by Bernd and Hilla Becher's photographs of industrial buildings, the designers reinterpreted these buildings in their functional installations.

GROWTH TABLE
TIM DURFEE AND IRIS ANNA REGN

Los Angeles-based architects Tim Durfee and Iris Anna Regn believe in the connective power of drawing as one of the truly universal activities. Their Growth Table (opposite) serves as a catalyst of spontaneous art-making: the cleverly constructed design welcomes users of all ages and sizes, and provides easy access to tools and surfaces for drawing – in other words, it has got all things necessary and sufficient to create 'an instant inter-generational community'.

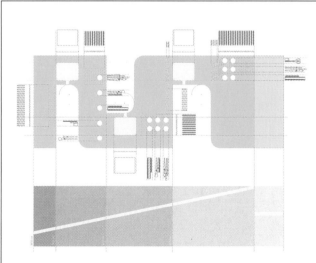

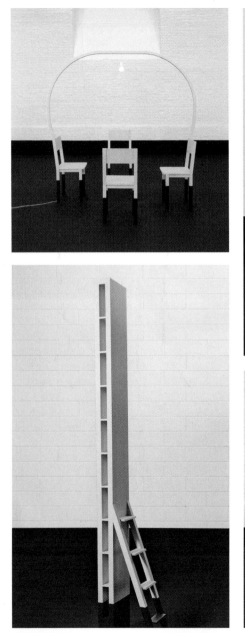
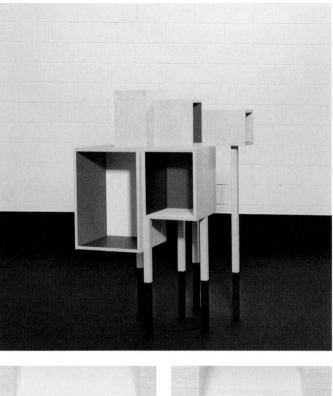
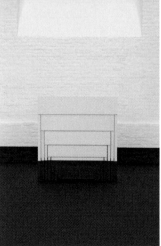
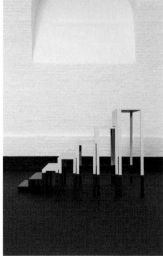

OBJET PRÉFÉRÉ
FABRICA

These designs (below and opposite) were among the results of a workshop that brought together young designers from Fabrica and fifteen employees of the Grand-Hornu Images cultural centre in Belgium. Favourite objects – from a chandelier to baby shoes, a personal library to renovated flats, a train to a laptop – were described through fifteen 'relational' installations that converted stories and memories into spatial signs.

PLATEAU
DANIEL LORCH

Plateau is industrial designer Daniel Lorch's alternative to a traditional desk. By extending the worktop both up- and downwards, he is able to free up more floor space. Although the desk only occupies a mere 0.4 m² (4 sq ft) in width, it offers an effective workspace of up to 1.6 m² (17 sq ft).

OBJET A, OBJET E, OBJET O
SEUNG-YONG SONG

The unconventional shapes of Korean designer Seung-Yong Song's enhanced chairs were the result, as he explains, of research into new potentials for interaction between objects and humans. Objet O (bottom left) is a hybrid of an armchair and an enormous paper lampshade that expands into a cocoon with varying degrees of privacy. Objet A (left) tops a chair with a few shelves, while Objet E (below) fuses a rocking chair and a clothes horse – an alternative to using a chair as a wardrobe.

SKIER
ANA BABIC

Serbian designer Ana Babic's hybrid Skier table (below) emerged from the need for a cleaner, better lit and more functional workplace. A task light is integrated into the table's structure, and has a panel fitted with an LED strip that runs the length of the desktop. Occupying a fraction of usable space, the lamp allows equal distribution of light over the working surface, and can be tilted at a convenient angle.

BED & STUDY
RASMUS B. FEX

For this project, Rasmus B. Fex wanted to create a debate about the lack of student housing. A house-shaped structure (above) offers just enough space for a collapsible desk and seat; at night, the only wall of this mini-house folds down to become a bed. As Fex explains: 'You need a place where you can be yourself and concentrate.'

BASE GVA OFFICE

GENEVA, SWITZERLAND
BUREAU A

With this design for a new office, compacted into a single, linear structure, architectural firm Bureau A brings rigorous geometry to the Gaudí-meets-Hundertwasser feel of Geneva's Schtroumpfs neighbourhood. Located in a 1980s building by Frei, Hunziker and Berthoud, the tiered arrangement creates a unique piece of furniture that functions as a library, a display for the work of the studio and a partition wall with twelve workstations lined up behind it.

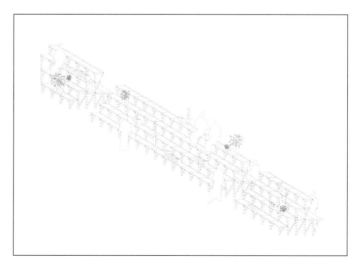

SPACE ORGANIZERS

WORKSHOP / BEHIND THE SCENES, ERIKSEN SKAJAA ARKITEKTER (P. 138)

AREA

ALAIN GILLES / MAGNITUDE.BE

With this project, Alain Gilles revised
the conventional concept of the bedroom
as a place to sleep. Here, the bed
becomes a focal point around which
other functions – bathroom, home office,
even a living room – are grouped.
The headboard is upgraded to a para-
architectural element that partitions
and structures the room, with its edges
treated as add-ons that can be bent at 90°
to create a semi-enclosed space behind.
The bed comes with a series of extra
elements, including two kinds of bedside
tables, a bench and hook-on lamp that
slides along the headboard.

PROOFF #002
WORKSOFA

STUDIO MAKKINK & BEY / PROOFF.COM

Organizing a space is also about organizing a process: WorkSofa by Studio Makkink & Bey was designed according to the premise that 'seating differently' can stimulate genuine dialogue. The design is modular and flexible, and suited to various socializing contexts: meetings, presentations, brainstorming sessions, group work, even 'a meeting with oneself'.

SOCIALIZING SOFAS

DITTE HAMMERSTRØM / ERIK-JOERGENSEN.COM

More conversation-encouraging furniture: this aerial view of Ditte Hammerstrøm's project illustrates how her sofa designs create a gently enclosed 'socializing archipelago'. Hybrids of back cushions and partitions provide friendly acoustics, cosiness and privacy, without disconnecting the user from the outside world.

UNKNOWN UNION
CAPE TOWN, SOUTH AFRICA
ARCHITECTURE AT LARGE

Intended as an antidote to 'dark and leathery' menswear store interiors, Unknown Union in Cape Town, designed by Rafael de Cárdenas of Architecture at Large, is a maze of ombré-painted display units, based on a cube matrix and extending across the ground floor of an eighteenth-century building. The architect 'gently negotiated' the interior spaces by creating freestanding display structures and cordoned-off pockets within the maze to accommodate dressing rooms and storage.

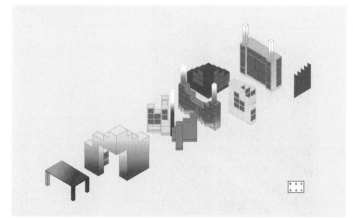

6T7 ESPAI CAFÉ
OLOT, SPAIN
MIQUEL SUBIRÀS

For this restaurant installation, architect and designer
Miquel Subiràs has created an atmospheric 'third place'
in the heart of Olot, in Catalonia. To optimize the use of the
compact L-shaped floor plan, Subiràs grouped all of the
functional elements of the bar into two austere, integrated
forms. 'We designed a piece of furniture to be perceived like
sculpture,' he says. 'Crafted from steel plates, it generates
pace and enhances the shape of the space.'

BAR DREIECK PARK

FUKUOKA, JAPAN
CASE-REAL

In this top-floor bar-with-a-view, designed by architect Koichi Futatsumata of Case-Real, drinkers' eyes can drift over the spectacular urban landscape or focus on the videos projected onto a wall just outside the window. The triangular shape of the oversized counter echoes that of the park outside, creating a similar void within. Futatsumata has modulated the width of the counter to enable different levels of intimacy between the customers and the bartender. In addition, this 'swollen counter' brings customers closer to the city view, while placing them at a comfortable distance from the projection wall. The backs of chairs, aligned with the counter top, and razor-thin disks of pendant lamps ensure that nothing blocks the view – inside or out.

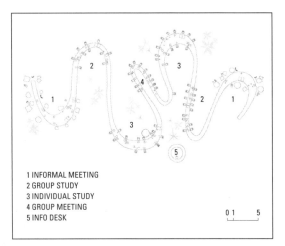

1 INFORMAL MEETING
2 GROUP STUDY
3 INDIVIDUAL STUDY
4 GROUP MEETING
5 INFO DESK

0 1   5

STUDY TABLE, CLOUD TABLE
STUDIO MAKS WITH PANG ARCHITECTS

Study Table (left and below) is the result of a collaboration between Studio MAKS and Pang Architects for the Chinese University Library, in Hong Kong. To improve spatial organization and bring the building in line with contemporary requirements, the team created a 'new study landscape': a 150 m (492 ft)-long table, which varies in height and width, morphing from a bank for informal meetings to a place for individual studies, via a group work table. Its successor, Cloud Table (opposite), was developed for Ventura Lambrate, a cluster of exhibitions held in Milan during the Salone del Mobile. Here, too, the designers explored the potential of tables for networking and information exchange.

Table Architecture #2
by STUDIO MAKS

1 INFO & CHARGING
2 PRESS
3 MEETING
4 WORKING & CHARGING
5 WIFI ZONE

0 1   5

BBDO CHILE
SANTIAGO, CHILE
OWAR ARQUITECTOS

A space divider designed by OWAR Arquitectos defines
a border between the work space and the circulation area
in BBDO Chile's offices. Comprising an array of modular units,
it condenses the storage needs of the entire department
into a single object, liberating the rest of the floor plan.
The modules slide along rails suspended from the ceiling
and guides incorporated in the floor, and the partition opens
and closes to let people in and out. Splitting the partition
wall into separate units also allows air and light into the
circulation zone, while maintaining the necessary distance
for manipulation of each module.

SALIRE
FUKUOKA, JAPAN
SINATO

This sculptural feature designed by architect Chikara Ohno of Sinato both dominates and organizes the interior of a fashion boutique in Fukuoka, Japan. L-shaped elements rotate around a central pivot; the lower ones act as display tables, while others incorporate clothing racks, mirrors and lighting. The units can be rearranged as new collections arrive, while the openness of the space in every direction is always maintained.

WORKSHOP / BEHIND THE SCENES
BERGEN, NORWAY
ERIKSEN SKAJAA ARKITEKTER

The new offices for the Bergen International Festival are contained in an open-plan space, whose workshop spirit informed the interior design by Norwegian architectural firm Eriksen Skajaa. Use of the premises shifts during the year from the planning phase to the festival period, when the number of both employees and activities increase. To accommodate these changing rhythms, the architects came up with a flexible solution, in which the wooden frameworks of mobile and permanent partitions convey the 'work-in-progress' feel. Placed behind prominent wooden structures, glass panels with concealed joints become virtually invisible, so that meeting rooms appear as open spaces. 'Shelf boxes' with integrated storage and benches are built around stairwells and provide nooks for one-on-one meetings or private phone calls.

HOUSE IN MEGUROHONCHO

TOKYO, JAPAN
TORAFU ARCHITECTS

Having re-purposed an old, mixed-use building into a house, Torafu Architects inserted a square aperture in the ceiling with a large multifunctional box directly underneath to connect the two upper floors. This cubic volume, with integrated stairs and built-in furniture (a bookcase, two wardrobes, a TV stand and a closet), is placed slightly off-centre, loosely dividing the open-plan room into spaces with different identities and functions. A landing at the top of the cube provides a small, interstitial space. A long, deep bay window that serves as a desk provides another 'furnitectural' element.

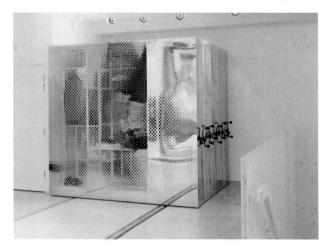

K-SPACE
LONDON, UK
6A ARCHITECTS

This concept store, designed by
6a Architects for sportswear brand
K-Swiss, can transform at a moment's
notice from a retail space into an open,
unbranded venue for cultural events.
Units containing a customized archive
system combine display and storage,
sliding on tracks to hide or reveal
their contents, which can be glimpsed
through perforations in the mirror-
polish surface.

CORNER PROJECT No2
STOCKHOLM, SWEDEN
GUISE ARCHITECTS

Of this project, the team at Swedish-based Guise Architects
say: 'We broke up the traditional sequence of rooms and
functions for a non-linear and non-hierarchical arrangement.
The previously strict spatial segregation of kitchen, living room
and bedrooms has been replaced by a forest of columns that
define the rooms. Since the apartment has no walls in the
traditional sense, spatiality is created by the pillars' relationship
to each other, rather than by clear physical boundaries.'

ROOM IN A ROOM

KOLORO-DESK, TORAFU ARCHITECTS (P. 148)

BRIEFCASE HOUSE
BUREAU SPECTACULAR

This project, located inside a 130 m²
(1,399 sq ft) loft with no partitions,
was conceived by Chicago-based
architectural firm Bureau Spectacular
as a house within a house. According
to architect Jimenez Lai, the design
'compacts the material possessions of
the client into one oversized briefcase, so
large that the client can sleep inside of it'.
Lai's project is a direct homage to Mies
van der Rohe's Farnsworth House (1951),
in Illinois, where the core of the building
produced 'four architectural programs,
without erecting one single wall'.

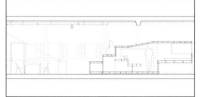

PROOFF #001 EAR CHAIR
STUDIO MAKKINK & BEY / PROOFF.COM

Originally conceived for the lobby of
Dutch insurance company Interpolis,
Studio Makkink & Bey's Ear chair creates
an island of privacy in the midst of
a public space. The large 'ears' provide
enclosure, while wide armrests double as
small tables. Two chairs pulled together
create a 'room'; a group of several
chairs with different ear lengths enable
a variety of spatial combinations.

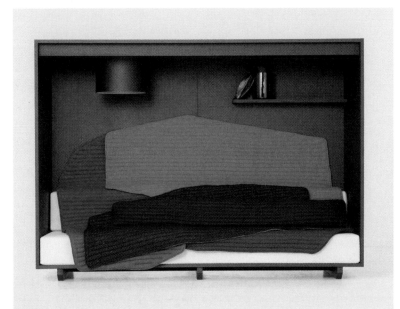

SOFA
RONAN AND ERWAN BOUROULLEC

This design by Ronan and Erwan
Bouroullec, developed for an exhibition
at Galerie Kreo, Paris, in 2008, blurs the
distinctions between space and object.
Both the configuration and the scale – 4
m × 2.2 m (13 ft × 7 ft) – make it difficult
to classify it as plain furniture. Instead
of fixed walls, the Bouroullec brothers
prefer more flexible arrangements,
such as textile partitions or a movable
alcove bed, to organize interior space
and provide privacy without setting
rigid and permanent limitations.

NAKED HOUSE
KAWAGOE, JAPAN
SHIGERU BAN ARCHITECTS

After being asked to design a house for a family that consisted of a couple, the husband's elderly mother, two young children and a dog, architect Shigeru Ban decided to take up the challenge when the client explained that the family wanted to reduce the amount of secluded spaces in order to encourage a spirit of togetherness, 'offering everyone the freedom to have individual activities in a shared atmosphere'. Ban's response was a vast, two-storey space, in which four individual 'rooms' are pushed about on casters. For heating or cooling, the rooms can be rolled closer to the heating or air-conditioning units, or simply pushed against the walls. The units can also be placed side by side to form a larger room, or taken out onto the terrace when it is necessary to free up the interior space. Additionally, the 'rooftops' of the mobile units can also serve as a supplementary playground for the children.

KOLORO-DESK

TORAFU ARCHITECTS / ICHIRODESIGN.JP

With 'windows' on each 'wall' and a 'skylight' in the 'ceiling', the Koloro-Desk (below), designed by Torafu Architects, provides an enclosure of sorts, with varying degrees of privacy and light. When open, small pull-down doors (the windows) on the sides of the desk function as shelves. To add to the multi-purpose remit, a stool does double-duty as a storage box.

ABITACOLO

BRUNO MUNARI / REXITE.COM

Transparent and enclosed at the same time, Abitacolo (above), Italian for cockpit, was conceived as a 'habitable module' for kids. The no-frills structure is a practical solution for smaller apartments, as it is easy to transport and assemble, weighing a mere 51kg (112 lbs), but it also provides, said the late architect Bruno Munari, 'a place to play, to sleep, to study and to have fun, a child's *hortus conclusus*, transformable at will'. First presented in 1971, now part of MOMA's permanent collection and back in production since 2013.

STUDIO HOUSE

BOLZANO, ITALY
HARRY THALER

When asked by the Museum of Modern and Contemporary Art in Bolzano to furnish their cube-shaped Studio House for resident artists and curators, Harry Thaler provided an interior design that conveys warmth, intimacy and comfort – a contrast to the glass and aluminium of the museum's exterior – while highlighting the space's workshop and study function. The furnishings include Thaler's take on a Murphy bed and canopy bed, with its own lighting, door, window and built-in wardrobe at the back, while the design of the desk is reminiscent of a large, panoramic picture window.

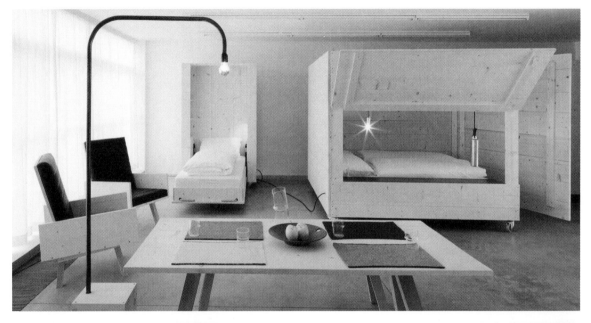

KENCHIKUKAGU
ATELIER OPA / TADAMOKKO.COM

Architect Toshihiko Suzuki of Atelier OPA explores intermediate concepts between furniture and architecture, or *kenchikukagu* (architectural furniture). Together with his team, Suzuki developed a series of 'foldaway rooms' (below and opposite), produced by Japanese firm Tadamokko, which aim to increase the capacity of our interiors and make them more flexible. The Foldaway Office is a solution for those who do not want to give up having a home office owing to lack of space, while the mobile Foldaway Kitchen does without exterior pipes and only needs to be plugged into an electric socket. The Foldaway Guest Room expands in width from 40 to 200 cm (16 to 79 in.) to provide guests with a bed, a mini-desk, a shelf and a lamp.

ORIGINAL CIRCLE KITCHEN
ALFRED AVERBECK / ORIGINAL-CIRCLE-KITCHEN.COM

Designer Alfred Averbeck's all-in-one, fully equipped kitchen (above) boasts a storage capacity of twelve cupboards, packed inside a revolving cylinder with sliding doors – all of this on a footprint of less than 1.8 m² (19 sq ft). The concept is both space- and effort-saving: the kitchen can be rotated to make objects come to the user, rather than the user having to move to reach them.

HI MATIC
PARIS, FRANCE
MATALI CRASSET

Designer Matali Crasset describes herself as a 'nest builder'.
In her Hi Matic hotel, nest-building begins in the lobby and
continues into the guest rooms, where, inspired by hostels and
Japanese *ryokans*, she designed wooden 'cabins' with add-ons,
including mini-desks. During the day, the cabin acts as a private
lounge; at night, an unfurled sleeping mat turns it into a bed.

SLEEPBOX
MOSCOW, RUSSIA
ARCH GROUP

The capsule hotel – the epitome of affordable hospitality in central locations – is now available in Moscow, thanks to the Sleepbox modules designed by Arch Group. On a 4 m² (43 sq ft) footprint, the 2.5 to 3 m (27 to 32 sq ft)-high Sleepboxes provide beds and storage space for one to three people, and can be installed anywhere associated with business travel, from exhibition centres to railway stations and airports.

PLUG-IN OFFICE

PHOENIX, ARIZONA
MARK RYAN STUDIO

Artist Louise Bourgeois's installation *Cells*, particularly the idea of 'solitude within groups', inspired architect Mark Ryan to design a transformable 'satellite office', set within a photographic studio in Phoenix, Arizona. The site was chosen for its 'active, energetic atmosphere' in the heart of the city's emerging arts district. 'There was a stated desire for some relief, or solitude, from this same dynamic environment for purposes of productivity and sanity,' Ryan explains. When not in use, the steel frame enclosure compacts to 2.1 × 4.3 m (7 × 14 ft), but can accommodate up to four people when deployed. Strategically placed shelf units block outward views when seated at the desk, but allow full participation with the space and activities when standing.

LPOVS
PARIS, FRANCE
37.2

Paris-based atelier 37.2 furnished a leasable photographic studio with a series of five mobile boxes, or 'micro-architectures', each intended for a particular task and outfitted accordingly – albeit always in a budget-conscious manner. The make-up and styling rooms are black boxes made of sheet steel, while two 'production cubes' of plywood have visually permeable walls for different effects: one is used as shelving; the other creates a relaxed veranda feel.

IN-BUILT

AESOP SAINT-HONORÉ, MARCH STUDIO (P. 163)

ARTIST STUDIO

TEL AVIV, ISRAEL
STUDIO RAANAN STERN

Dozens of '2D treasures' collected by one artist and her family over seventy years are cleverly stored and arranged in this compact atelier-cum-guestroom. 'Each piece was measured, organized and ordered according to groups, sizes and artistic connections,' explains architect Raanan Stern. The organizational stage led to four basic proportions, which determined the parameters of the wall's cells, cupboards and drawers. Pull-out sections for displaying and storing artworks, tools and materials can be removed and placed on the work table as necessary. A removable sliding door acts as a display board or easel, and conceals a guest bed.

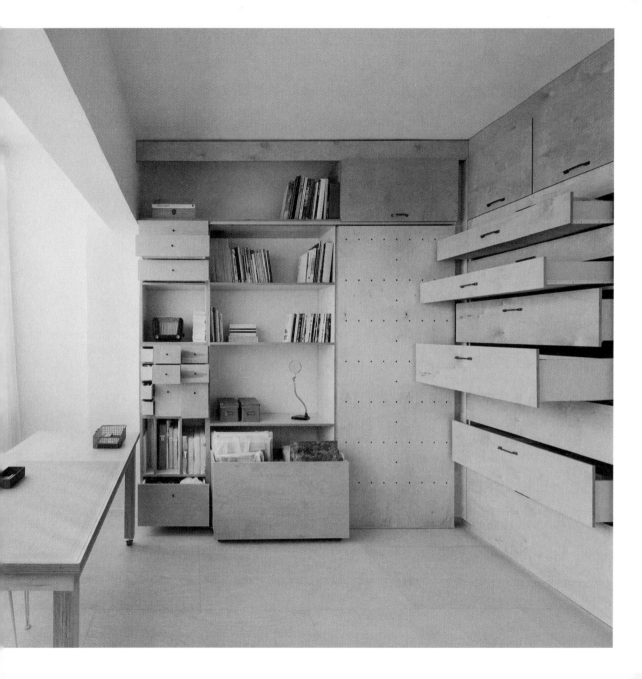

SAMUEL KUNG

HONG KONG, CHINA
EDGE DESIGN INSTITUTE

The design solution for this jewelry shop was guided by two conditions: the use of the Penrose tiling pattern (an iconic element of the brand's identity), and allowance for the installation of a floor painting after completion of the interior works. Architect Gary Chang of Edge Design Institute suggested a 'brutal yet logical design strategy', in which the interior would be designed to 'leave the ground clear'. The walls and ceiling form a single lattice to screen exterior light, creating an ambiance appropriate for the display of jewelry. Altering the Penrose pattern slightly, Chang produced a three-dimensional wall, in which a series of folds added rigidity to the surface, and enabled showcases to be inserted into the distorted cubic volumes.

MON PETIT

ESCALDES-ENGORDANY, ANDORRA
MIQUEL MERCE AND MIQUEL SUBIRÀS

For Andorra's first shop selling vintage goods for babies, architects Miquel Merce and Miquel Subiràs had to develop a display system suitable for both large and small items, and to balance the energetic colours of children's toys and clothes with an orderly, no-frills presentation. A mono-material solution – black plates of recycled steel, arranged along the walls like a macro-barcode – does both jobs. Product shelves are set between the vertical plates, inviting customers to engage with the space. When viewed from the side, the steel blades appear opaque and heavy; from the front, they dematerialize and focus attention on the products, skilfully highlighted by the dark, subtly reflective steel.

MAGIC STORE

TOKYO, JAPAN
TORAFU ARCHITECTS

Magic Store sells contact lenses in ultra-slim packaging developed by the Japanese brand Menicon. To celebrate this unique technology, Torafu Architects chose to display the products across a ribbed surface, with the merest hint of shelving. The smooth wall is curved around the store; the depth and height of its extrusions and recesses reflect the dimensions of the packaging. The entire wall acts as a canvas on which the products can be placed virtually anywhere; from the street, the store appears as one large, white showcase.

AESOP SAINT-HONORÉ

PARIS, FRANCE
MARCH STUDIO

For its flagship store in Paris, Australian brand Aesop chose
an eighteenth-century building in the heart of the city.
Designer Rodney Eggleston of March Studio searched for
a material that would be in keeping with the local architecture,
and, intrigued by the parquetry floors seen throughout Paris,
he suggested 'inhabiting the space with one material, used in
one encompassing way'. A total of 3,500 pieces of timber were
processed in Melbourne, meticulously numbered and shipped
to France to form the store's floor, walls and ceiling, as well
as the integrated shelving and counters.

MODEL APARTMENT

NEW YORK, NEW YORK
SMITH-MILLER + HAWKINSON ARCHITECTS

For this conceptual design for a New York apartment, architectural firm Smith-Miller + Hawkinson explored the machine-for-living quality of the space by replacing the main partition wall with a double-height cabinet that incorporates 'everything needed to live in the city: pull-out bed, bookshelves, closets and a pegged wall for storage and display'. Gerrit Rietveld's Schröder House and Pierre Chareau's Maison de Verre are cited as inspirations, as is *Door: 11, rue Larrey* by Marcel Duchamp, in which a single door is used to alternately close off one of the two adjacent rooms.

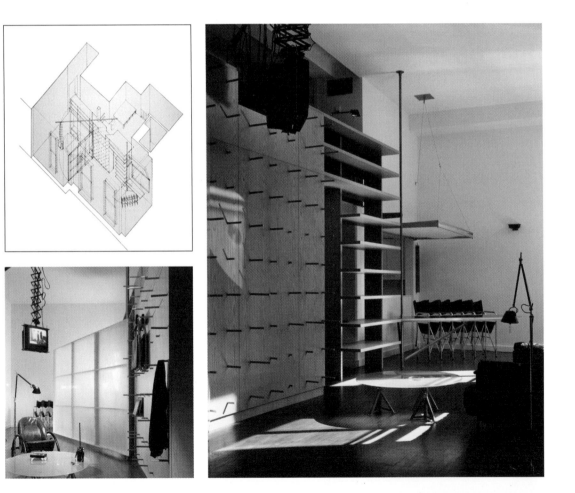

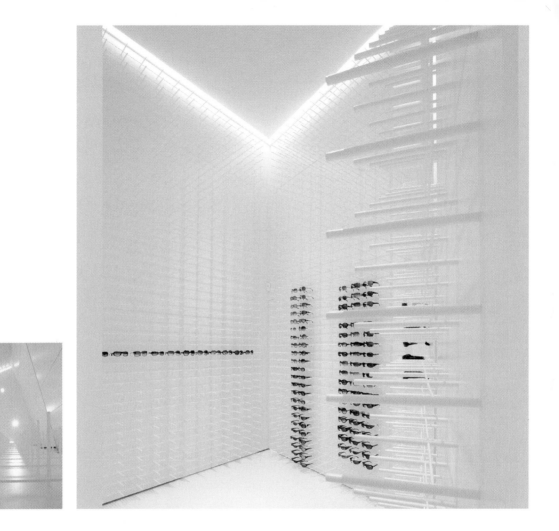

VANITY
GENK, BELGIUM
KARLA MENTEN ARCHITECTURE AND BASSAM EL OKEILY

Architects Bassam El Okeily and Karla Menten designed this 40 m² (431 sq ft) retail interior as a comment on vanity – a reflection on the shop's key product: designer sunglasses. While the first of the two rooms contains only mirrors and quotes on the subject of vanity, the second is a 'temple of consumption': its 5.4 m (18 ft)-high walls are lined, floor to ceiling, with uniform white rods that act as a product display.

600% STORAGE

NEW YORK, NEW YORK
MODU

For a flat belonging to a newlywed couple, Phu Hoang and Rachely Rotem of architectural practice MODU created the 'equivalent of an extra bedroom, without sacrificing valuable floor area'. The result – a six-fold storage space – also needed to cope with some additional challenges. Since one half of the couple prefers to store his belongings out of sight and the other likes to display her things on open shelves, the architects catered to the pair's contrasting needs by designing a wall system that provides both hidden storage space and multiple shelves, like a series of mantelpieces, around the fireplace.

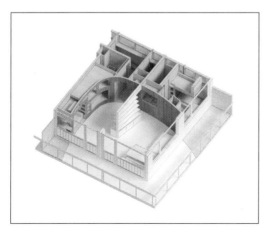

THE CABIN

LES MENUIRES, FRANCE
H2O ARCHITECTES

At a ski resort in France, Paris-based h2o Architectes faced the seemingly impossible task of creating increased living space without affecting the structural elements, adding two bathrooms and accommodating eight beds in an area measuring only 55 m² (592 sq ft). The team's solution was to 'invert the perspective': rather than fitting the furniture into the apartment, they fit the apartment into the furniture. A curved wooden wall provides structure and divides the building into two parts; bunk beds, kitchen, bathroom and storage areas are docked into it at the rear, creating space in front for a large living room with a panoramic mountain view.

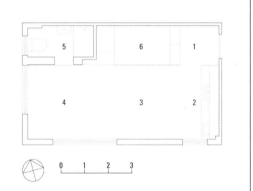

THE STUDIO

SYDNEY, AUSTRALIA
NICHOLAS GURNEY

1 ENTRY FOYER / 2 KITCHEN / 3 DINING ROOM
4 LIVING ROOM / 5 BATHROOM / 6 BEDROOM

Architect Nicholas Gurney's redesign of a 27 m² (291 sq ft) studio in Sydney is a 'proposal for future high-density urban living for one-person families, the fastest growing demographic'. Built in four weeks with a budget of less than Aus$40,000, the design addresses the tricky issues inherent to micro-apartments: lack of privacy, storage and living space. An integrated 'joinery pod' condenses the essential functions into less than half of the footprint, conserving light and preserving the city view. Wall-to-wall sliding doors change the function of the studio space from sleeping to living/dining modes.

DRAWER HOUSE
TOKYO, JAPAN
NENDO

Japanese design office Nendo suggests a housing solution
that can be applied to Tokyo, as well as to any city where space
is at a premium. On both storeys of their Drawer House,
all 'residential functions' are concealed inside a single wall
on one side of the room, 'and can be pulled out when necessary,
like drawers'.

GARY'S APARTMENT

HONG KONG, CHINA
EDGE DESIGN INSTITUTE

In this design for his own flat, Gary Chang of Edge Design Institute combines high density and high intensity in an area of only 4 × 8 m (13 × 26 ft). This interactive home is 'an experiment in putting all the essential domestic activities into one compact space, without compromising lifestyle choices'. To maintain living standards in an extremely limited space, Chang explores the 'smart use of resources in space and time'. Functions that are not in use are compressed in layers around the perimeter and unfolded or pulled out one at a time. As a result, this transformer apartment adapts to the user's needs so that the space available for each function becomes larger than would normally be expected.

LANDSCAPES

NEIL BARRETT

TOKYO, JAPAN
ZAHA HADID ARCHITECTS

The rigour and audacity of Zaha Hadid's design for the Neil Barrett flagship store in Tokyo are rooted in the fashion brand's signature style: minimal cut, plus 'fixed points, folding, pleating and cut-outs'. Two architectural-scale installations in thermoformed Corian dominate the mens- and womenswear sections, with their complex surfaces 'unravelling and folding to form the shelving display and seating'. The smooth finish of these semi-geological formations is offset by raw concrete, while the matt whiteness of the Corian is accentuated by the contrast with the glossy black floor.

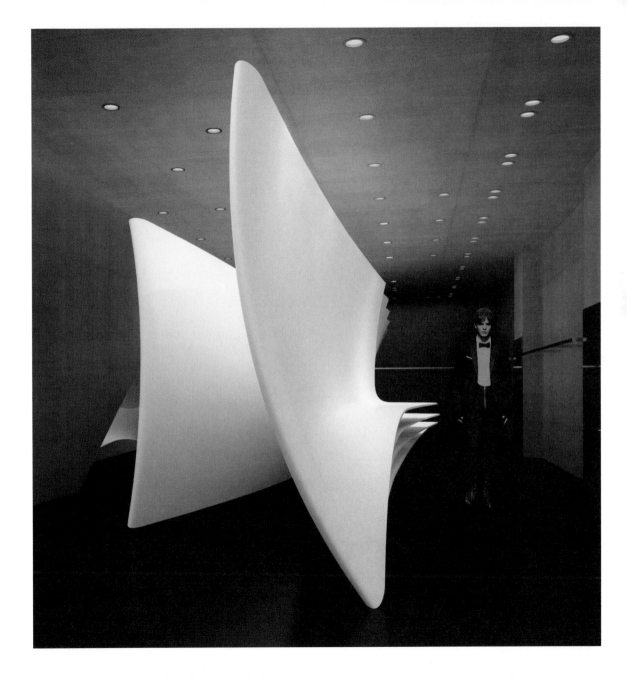

RICHARD CHAI

NEW YORK, NEW YORK
SNARKITECTURE

This temporary retail installation for designer Richard Chai
was part of the annual Building Fashion series, initiated by
Boffo and pairing fashion designers with architects to create
temporary retail installations. The 2010 event was sited beneath
the High Line in New York, inside the former sales trailer for Neil
Denari's HL23 building. The architects displayed the garments
in 'a glacial cavern, carved from the confines of the existing
structure', while a landscape of 'erosions and extensions' was
shaped from architectural foam blocks, with display niches and
hanging rails embedded in the sculptural volumes.

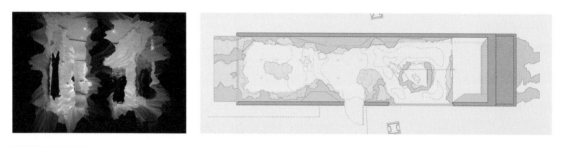

LUNA
CLAESSON KOIVISTO RUNE / DUNE-NY.COM

Luna, by Claesson Koivisto Rune, has been described by
manufacturers Dune as a 'large crater-like surface designed
for exploration … sometimes referred to as super-furniture',
presenting it as a landscape that can also function as an
individual piece. Even the designers themselves are unsure
whether the Swiss cheese-holed design is a piece of furniture,
a small house or 'an upholstered playground for grown-ups'.

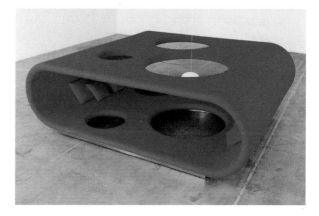

RADIO NEXT

MOSCOW, RUSSIA
SL*PROJECT

By placing a broadcasting studio behind a soundproof glass wall, architectural firm SL*Project put the workings of Moscow radio station Radio Next on display in a shopping centre (below). An elevated floor both formed a stage for the crew and concealed the cabling, while the DJ's workstation and seats for presenters and guests were connected into a single irregular, ribbon-like feature made out of Corian, whose complex angular topography improved the room's acoustic properties.

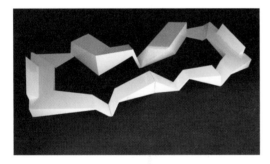

LE VIGNE

NEW YORK, NEW YORK
MADLAB WITH SPURSE

For this budget-savvy remodelling of a 56 m² (603 sq ft) wine shop in New York's Greenwich Village (above), architects MADLAB 'transformed stockpiles of recycled furniture into a unique retail environment for artisanal Italian wines'. Together with design consultancy Spurse, the team dismembered and reassembled second-hand tables to form an 8 m (26 ft)-long centrepiece that 'displays and stores wine in nooks and clusters, as if moving through the country's wine regions from north to south'.

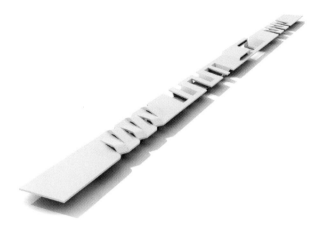

THE WORLD'S LONGEST TABLE
FOR ALL CULTURES
UNSTUDIO

The team at Amsterdam-based architectural firm UNStudio set their minds to designing a table suited for all sorts of scenarios, from solo uses to formal meetings for bigger groups. This demo piece, 55 m (180 ft) long and 2.6 m (9 ft) wide, is a modular system composed of segments with various functions, including a coffee bar that is seamlessly blended into the overall landscape. It was shown at the 2008 IMM Furniture Fair in Cologne.

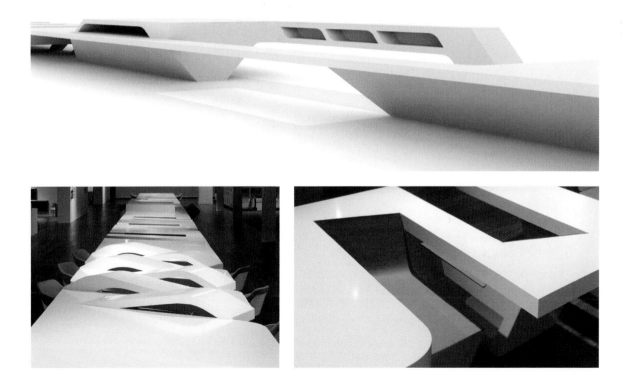

CIRCLE
UNSTUDIO / WALTERKNOLL.DE

This design for a sofa by UNStudio is based on the shape
of a circle, but is not limited to a single configuration. The
piece splits into three parts that can be arranged into sculptural
forms. The height of the backrest is fixed, while its gradually
varied slope allows for different seating modes, from upright
to reclined.

DUNE FORMATIONS
ZAHA HADID ARCHITECTS

For this project, created for London-based David Gill Galleries
and shown at the Venice Biennale in 2007, shelves, tables
and benches were 'redefined into abstractions leading
to a unique interpretation of an interior landscape'. Architect
Zaha Hadid transcended the familiar language of verticals and
horizontals through her signature use of dynamic geometries,
advanced 3D modelling and digital fabrication.

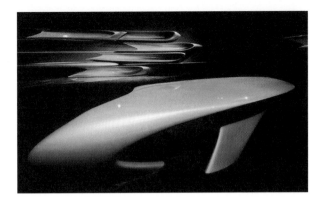

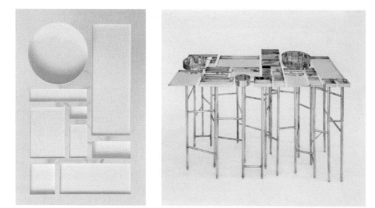

OCD
HÉCTOR ESRAWE / ESRAWE.COM

For this project, called OCD (for obsessive compulsive disorder), Mexican designer Héctor Esrawe divided a tabletop into a series of small, walled trays in various sizes, each perched on its own upright. Grouped together, the collection forms 'an inventory of everyday objects, describing the habits and preferences of their owners and reflecting their identities'.

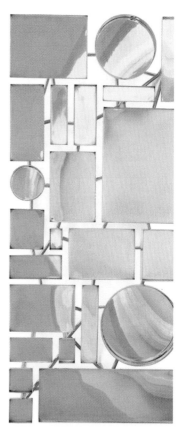

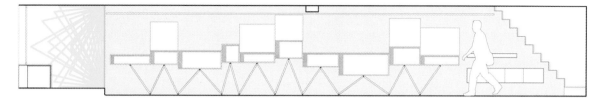

SEVENSISTERS
BASEL, SWITZERLAND
ZMIK

The long, narrow footprint and constantly updated product range of the Sevensisters concept store, in Basel, guided the designers at ZMIK in their concept for a bespoke display system, which combines the qualities of a table and shelf. The team describe the result as 'ten individual volumes, which form one continuous, completely white display topography, balanced on shared sets of legs'. Colourful products are presented both on top of and inside the display pieces, with the top of each unit opening up to provide more options.

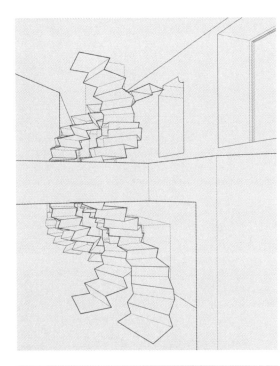

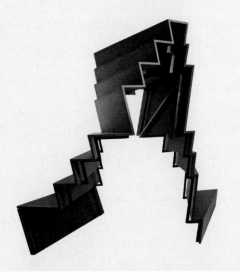

FIFTH AVENUE SHOE REPAIR

STOCKHOLM, SWEDEN
GUISE ARCHITECTS

For Swedish fashion brand Fifth Avenue Shoe Repair, Guise Architects were asked to produce a striking yet commercially viable retail interior – one that would offer 'a spatial encounter with the brand'. Looking at the company's design method through an architectural lens, the team revised the form and function of a familiar typology, turning a black staircase with a double-helix twist into a display unit. As architect Andreas Ferm explains: 'Since the main form is folded and rotated, it conceals and exposes the products as one moves through the store.'

SPAR FLAGSHIP STORE
BUDAPEST, HUNGARY
LAB5

Challenged to design a unique interior for a new Spar supermarket in central Budapest, architectural firm LAB5 looked to the store's customer flow to come up with spatial and formal solutions. The team created an 'expressway' for those who grab a sandwich on the run, a 'short route' for daily purchases, and a long one for weekend shopping. The wine section, a 3D environment in plywood lamellae, is a highlight: its sculpture-meets-function morphology embraces the ceiling, continues down the walls and drips onto the floor to form freestanding displays.

DIAMEDIA MINDS OFFICE

HASSELT, BELGIUM
KARLA MENTEN ARCHITECTURE

In order to turn a narrow space that only had windows
on two short walls into a creative headquarters for a marketing
office, architect Karla Menten rejected traditional partitions
and instead raised the floor to table height. This arrangement
provides a workspace for six to eight people, lockers,
archives, a computer-server room and a kitchenette, with
meeting rooms fishbowled behind curved glass walls.
A palette of pristine white maximizes light reflection, and
contributes to the feeling of spaciousness.

KU 64

BERLIN, GERMANY
GRAFT ARCHITECTS

Helping dental patients to let go
of their fears in a relaxing, spa-like
environment was the concept behind
Graft Architects' design for the KU 64
dental clinic in Berlin. The intimidating,
sterile atmosphere normally associated
with a dentist's office has been replaced
by an architectural take on a seaside
landscape, with treatment rooms set
behind yellow 'dunes'. In the children's
wing, note the architects, topographic
features 'drip from the ceiling,
inverting the dune typology to become
elements that can be climbed onto
and into for play or privacy'.

ALICE EUPHEMIA
MELBOURNE, AUSTRALIA
EDWARDS MOORE

On the architects' to-do list for a new design for the Alice Euphemia boutique (left) in Melbourne was to encourage shoppers to explore every corner; create a magnetic, 'otherworldly' atmosphere; and maximize retail opportunities at the shop, which is devoted to showcasing Australian fashion talents. The key design element is a 'terrain', which connects the store's two levels and provides a flexible display that extends the full height of the space. Its timber steps support mannequins and acrylic display boxes, while providing glimpses of a cave-like area beneath, where more garment designs are on offer.

BLUEFROG MUSIC CLUB
MUMBAI, INDIA
SERIE ARCHITECTS

The concept for an acoustic lounge for blueFROG (opposite) was to collapse a theatre, restaurant, bar and club into a smoothly functioning amalgamation, with a premium sound experience to top it off – all within a former industrial warehouse. Chris Lee and Kapil Gupta of Serie Architects responded with an undulating cellular structure of circular booths built around a stage. The height of the structure increases away from the stage, affording uninterrupted views of the performances.

DURAS DAIBA
TOKYO, JAPAN
SINATO

At this boutique within a shopping mall in Tokyo, designer Chikara Ohno of Sinato has made use of the whole of the store's 3.65 m (12 ft) height by inserting a second display area in expanded metal mesh, suspended at 2.25 m (7 ft) and accessible via two stepped platforms built out of concrete slabs. From the top of these two 'hills', shoppers can reach 'beyond the clouds', where mirror-clad walls create the illusion of infinity.

SHUN*SHOKU LOUNGE

OSAKA, JAPAN
KENGO KUMA & ASSOCIATES

For the 82 m² (883 sq ft) Shun*Shoku Lounge, an installation
for restaurant guide Gurunavi, Kengo Kuma piled up slices of
plywood to form an interior landscape, comprising reception
desk, bar counter, seats and shelves. The space serves
as a public-relations area and information booth; the layered
configuration of panels recalls the V&A Museum of Design,
in Dundee, Scotland, also conceived by Kuma.

3

SYNTHESIS

In 1925, Friedrich Kiesler designed Raumstadt (City in Space), as both exhibition furniture and an architectural model to describe a new concept of the city. His vision included urban blocks, hovering above the ground, and the 'living buildings' liberated from walls and foundations, embracing the entire diversity of our activities.

'Furnitectural thinking' brings together innovators whose ideas are ahead of their time, and vernacular solutions that seem to have always been there – from the Breton box bed, revisited in 2000 by Ronan and Erwan Bouroullec, to the traditional Russian stove. Intended for single-room houses, the former allowed for both warmth and a certain amount of privacy. A wooden chest of the same length performed the triple function of seating, storage and access to the bed above. Similarly, the architecture of the Russian stove allows for heating and cooking, as well as a place for sleeping. These multipurpose objects act as space-makers, enabling interaction and privacy, and creating tools and conditions for using a small space with maximum intensity.

The borderland where furniture and architecture meet creates an organic whole that expands in different directions. Architectural historian Kenneth Frampton described Pierre Chareau's Maison de Verre (1928–32) as 'a grossly enlarged piece of furniture, interjected into an altogether larger realm' – a description that could also be applied to the projects featured in 'Architectural Shelving' and 'Macro-furniture', whether Neri & Hu's showroom in Shanghai (p. 212) or Graft's loft apartment in Hamburg (p. 210).

Each of these projects is a 'functional cluster', where the container and the content are not separated, but rather co-design each other, such as MVRDV's Book Mountain (p. 216) in Spijkenisse, Netherlands, Edge Design Institute's Suitcase House (p. 202) in Beijing, Moussafir Architects' solution for a partition-free dwelling in Paris (p. 226) or OLK I RÜF's concept for a mixed-use building in downtown Vienna (p. 224).

The examples in 'Partitions' look at the ways in which design projects can contribute to the larger task of creating fluid, flexible domestic and working spaces that change in synch with our lives. 'Plug-ins & Add-ons' and 'Building Blocks' revisit modular and parametric design, this time applied at the scale of architectural objects. A house gets deconstructed into an assembly kit of prefab units, each shaped to perform a specific function: clients are invited to configure their own bespoke homes, and user input materializes into a remarkable spatial experience. Playing cards, toys and geometrical grids provide ideas for structural systems, successfully used in furniture and buildings alike, sometimes in a two-in-one combination.

And to wrap up the story, 'Multi-scale' highlights cases in which designers and architects develop transversal methods, where buildings and furniture seem to be a consequence of larger experiments with three-dimensionality and movement.

MACRO-FURNITURE

SUITCASE HOUSE
BEIJING, CHINA
EDGE DESIGN INSTITUTE

Part of Commune by the Great Wall, an experimental development in Beijing, this project by Edge Design Institute 'attempts to rethink the nature of intimacy, privacy, spontaneity and flexibility … blurring the boundaries between house, interior and furniture'. The approach enables infinite scenarios, from a solitary retreat to a series of suites, and from a configuration adapted to maximum daytime activities (kitchen and dining room, library and study, games area and a cinema) to a multi-bedroom arrangement at night. Architect Gary Chang notes that the building was constructed as a stacking of layers, with the middle layer containing general activities and flow. Mobile partitions transform this 44 × 5 m (144 × 16 ft) space according to the number of guests, activities and degrees of privacy. The bottom layer is a container for dedicated 'compartments', concealed by pneumatically assisted floor panels to open only when required.

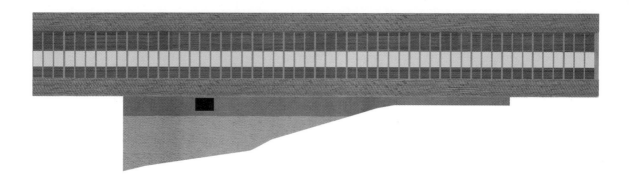

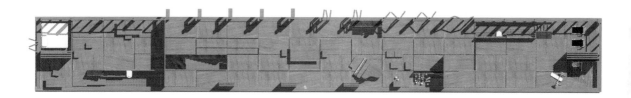

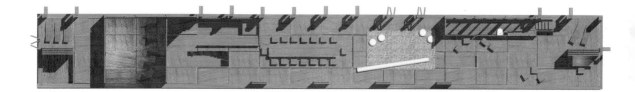

TEXTILE PAVILION
LUXEMBOURG CITY, LUXEMBOURG
RONAN AND ERWAN BOUROULLEC

For this restaurant and shop for the Musée d'Art Moderne Grand-Duc Jean, in Luxembourg, Ronan and Erwan Bouroullec had to enable a sheltered space beneath the museum's glass roof to offer protection from the strong light, both direct and reflected off the floor. The brothers responded with two 'autonomous human-scale architectures' that breach the 'vertical geometry … to create an atmosphere of home comfort'. Transparent yet robust wooden structures, covered by a skin made of textile tiles (see p. 234), provide both shade and conversation-friendly acoustics.

RECLAIM

LÉOPOLD BANCHINI AND HARRY GUGGER / RECLAIM.BH

For Bahrain's entry at the 2010 Architecture Biennale in Venice, six researchers, a film director and a photographer explored how decades of land reclamation and urban expansion brought about the decline of the country's traditional seafaring culture. In designing the exhibition, architects Léopold Banchini of Bureau A and Harry Gugger relied on 'experiencing, rather than observing', using three fishermen's huts, ejected from their original context and transported to Venice, to tell a story of disruption.

WALDEN

NILS HOLGER MOORMANN

The concept of simple living described by Henry David Thoreau in *Walden, or Life in the Woods* (1854) inspired Nils Holger Moormann to design a piece of mega-furniture of extraordinary proportions, amply equipped for the outdoor life. It contains an in-built gazebo (complete with a sun blind), a ladder for accessing the rooftop sun deck, a fold-down picnic table, a lamp, even a birdhouse, while its compartments and niches provide storage space for gardening tools and grill utensils, a hanging cooking pot and firewood.

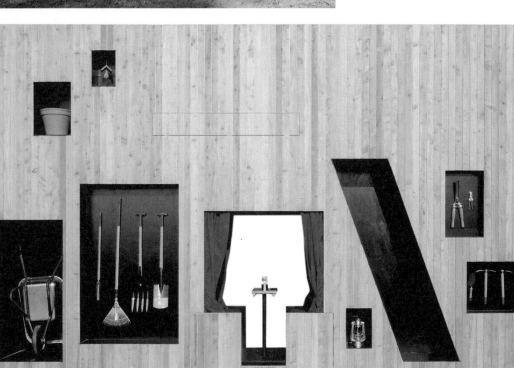

TA ĐI ÔTÔ
HANOI, VIETNAM
BUREAU A

'Everything is dense in Hanoi, everything is made use of,' note the team at Bureau A. 'Things live different lives; they reincarnate continuously into new functions, passing from one life to another without a moment of respite.' The designers' own contribution to this grass-roots creativity is a piece of itinerant architecture-meets-furniture, 'conceived as an ephemeral house or a vertical street food restaurant', an object that could deviate from its original function and become something else: a mini-concert stage or a poets' podium, to be determined while cruising the busy streets of the Vietnamese capital.

GRAPH

BEIJING, CHINA
RINTALA EGGERTSSON ARCHITECTS

Designed by Sami Rintala, Dagur Eggertsson and Vibeke Jenssen for the National Art Museum of China, Graph is a versatile solution for an emergency shelter, serving both small and large groups of people. Modular units add up to a fully functional one- or two-storey building, and the space-efficient pods for sleeping, cooking, storage and sanitary purposes can be organized in various ways. This flexibility makes it possible to adapt the shelters to the needs of individual families, as well as to different climates, social patterns and cultural traditions.

PENTHOUSE ON THE LOIRE

NANTES, FRANCE
AVIGNON-CLOUET ARCHITECTES

Architects Benjamin Avignon and Saweta Clouet designed this top-floor loft as a series of functional clusters within one shared space, where the inhabitants would feel as if they were 'constantly immersed in the landscape'. One such cluster is a micro-architectural object comprising a sequence of places for work, play, entertaining, cooking, eating, washing up and storage. Another, more contained unit is an array of white, round-edged metal closets that house a bed, bookcase and study.

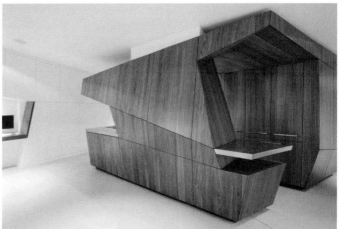

LOFT HAMBURG

HAMBURG, GERMANY
GRAFT ARCHITECTS

For a loft apartment in Hamburg, the team at Graft produced a furnitectural solution that arose from the need to integrate existing fixed utilities into the new design. The related functions (kitchen, bath and toilet) are compressed into a freestanding, walnut-panelled block; openings cut into the monolithic volume let daylight deeper into the living space. The 'service walls' along the perimeter of the loft have niches for more flexible functions, such as working, sleeping or lounging.

CAMPER SHOWROOM

SHANGHAI, CHINA
NERI & HU DESIGN AND RESEARCH OFFICE

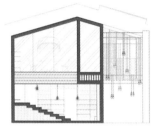

Lyndon Neri and Rossana Hu reinterpreted the vernacular urban landscape in this design for a showroom for footwear brand Camper. Taking their cue from the spatial characteristics of Shanghai's *nong tang* alleys, they extended one such passageway inside a former warehouse, where it slashes through a small building and opens it up in a sectional cut to reveal the showroom space. Having experienced the layering of exterior, interior and in-between areas, clients then venture into the dissected structure. Inserted within the shell of the existing warehouse, this two-storey building-as-furniture has a timber frame, which occasionally doubles as shoe display, and an infill of bricks and salvaged wood sourced from demolished lane houses.

ARK BOOK TOWER

LONDON, UK
RINTALA EGGERTSSON ARCHITECTS

For the exhibition '1:1 Architects Build Small Spaces', held
at the Victoria & Albert Museum, Sami Rintala, Dagur
Eggertsson and Vibeke Jenssen designed the Ark, intended
as a call to slow down and look into the issues of nature
preservation and biodiversity 'from the inside'. The freestanding
structure towered above the stairwell of the museum's National
Art Library, inviting visitors to retreat to the single-person
reading room at its core. Titles are only visible when inside;
to passers-by, the books look like white bricks.

LIYUAN LIBRARY
JIAOJIEHE, CHINA
LI XIAODONG

When asked to design a library for a small village near Beijing, architect Li Xiaodong chose to build it off the village centre, on a beautiful site that felt particularly conducive to contemplation. In keeping with the desire for the project to blend with nature, humble deadwood sticks used by the villagers to fuel their ovens served as cladding for the façade and to soften the bright daylight entering the fully glazed library. The interior is a single piece of macro-furniture: the wooden structure doubles as a huge bookcase, with a combination of steps, platforms and storage compartments placing readers right among the books and carefully framed landscape views.

BOOK MOUNTAIN

SPIJKENISSE, NETHERLANDS
MVRDV

For a community in the western Netherlands with 10 per cent illiteracy, Dutch architectural firm MVRDV designed Book Mountain as 'an advert for reading'. The glass exterior and the architecture of the bookshelves, together with the central location, make the library visible from everywhere. This powerful symbol was made possible by the building's organizational structure, with non-library functions, including retail, offices and auditorium, compacted inside the pyramidal base, which, in turn, supports the platforms that house the library's bookshelves.

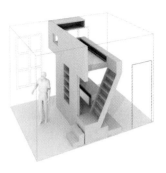

EVA'S BED

PARIS, FRANCE
H2O ARCHITECTES

The arrival of a second baby prompted
a young couple to think of ways
to provide both of their children with
a personal space. Dividing the children's
room in two seemed an obvious solution,
but the team at h2o Architectes had
a better idea. Instead of a simple
partition, they built an entire new room
folded into a playful furniture hybrid.
In addition to the requisite elements,
including a bed, a desk and a (secret)
storage space, this multipurpose space
contains stairs, cavities and niches
for climbing, hiding and other, yet-to-be-
discovered activities.

UFOGEL

NUSSDORF-DEBANT, AUSTRIA
PETER JUNGMANN WITH ABERJUNG DESIGN AGENCY

Part UFO, part *vogel* (German for bird), this East Tyrolean
holiday house by Peter Jungmann and Aberjung Design Agency
accommodates up to five people within its 45 m² (484 sq ft)
footprint. Built from larch timber, UFOgel's smart construction
offers both openness and protection. The space-saving,
light-filled interior is largely defined by the building's sculptural
form and multipurpose furniture units, which are integrated
into the architecture.

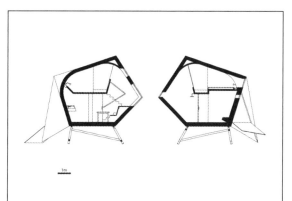

ROLLING STONES

GRAZ, AUSTRIA
INNOCAD ARCHITEKTUR ZT GMBH

In the design for a new information centre for a tourist office in Graz, Austria, occupying the Cannon Room in the seventeenth-century Styrian Armoury building, cobblestone becomes the key element of spatial branding. The team at multidisciplinary firm INNOCAD Architektur found that the material, which forms the geological base of the city and provides the foundations of its historic buildings and paving, lends its organic shape to the reception desk, shop, ticket counter and information booth. Individual pods are defined by a three-dimensional 'space-forming grid', which blends structure and furniture (counters, display shelves, storage). The pods are lined up beneath the building's vaulted ceilings, and are open or enclosed according to their function.

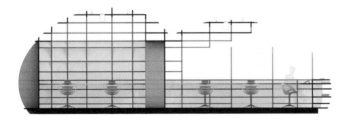

ARCHITECTURAL SHELVING

JOSÉ VASCONCELOS LIBRARY, TALLER DE ARQUITECTURA X (P. 228)

KRAMERGASSE 13

VIENNA, AUSTRIA
OLK | RÜF

This project is a proposal for a mixed-use office and residential building in downtown Vienna. Given its tight footprint, architects Oskar Leo Kaufmann and Albert Rüf needed to find a way to declutter the floor plan. To do so, they designed a glass façade, whose load-bearing structure functions as full-height shelving and incorporates heating, water ducts for the sprinkler system, anti-glare shielding, blinds and natural ventilation.

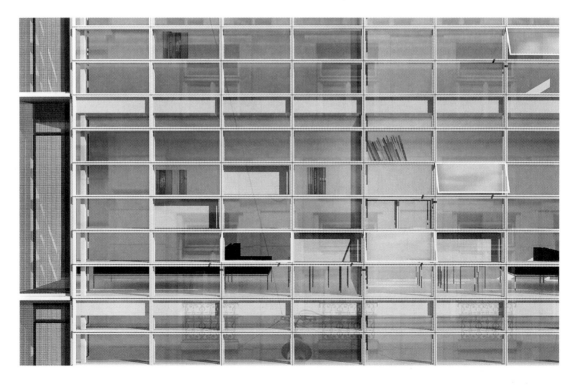

HOUSE T
TOKYO, JAPAN
HIROYUKI SHINOZAKI ARCHITECTS

Located in central Tokyo, this
residence-cum-atelier was designed
as an oversized bookcase, with floor
plates for shelves. Architect Hiroyuki
Shinozaki enhanced this shelving effect
by leaving large openings between
the adjacent rooms. Vertical elements
are reduced to cross-shaped supporting
pillars and lightweight stairs, creating
an extraordinary visual depth
in all directions and the impression
of living on a stage.

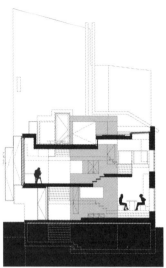

MAISON ESCALIER

PARIS, FRANCE
MOUSSAFIR ARCHITECTES

Strictly speaking, Maison Escalier, or Staircase House, is a single room that extends from the basement to the top floor. As the client required a house with a generous sense of space, natural lighting and no partition walls, Moussafir Architectes designed a tree-like structure with floor plates branching off the central stem. The entire house is structured as one huge staircase: its core integrates the kitchen and two bathrooms, while its steps and landings contain a fluid sequence of living spaces. The timber cladding, uniformly applied to the central core, floors and ceilings, reinforces the design concept. Concrete cases mounted on masonry walls serve as built-in storage. While the house was conceived as one large piece of wooden furniture, these concrete storage items appear as architectural elements.

JOSÉ VASCONCELOS LIBRARY
MEXICO CITY, MEXICO
TALLER DE ARQUITECTURA X

Behind this project for the José Vasconcelos Library in Mexico City, designed by Alberto Kalach of Taller de Arquitectura X, was the idea of the library as an ark of knowledge. Books are gathered in the centre of the building, within an independent steel and glass structure that stretches along its length like a spinal column. This six-storey-high feature seems to float above the main lobby; a system of pathways and stairs allows browsers to travel inside the giant bookcase, which can store over one and a half million volumes.

AMIDA HOUSE

SHIZUOKA, JAPAN
KOCHI ARCHITECT'S STUDIO

Amida House by Kazuyasu Kochi is Le Corbusier's Dom-ino system revisited and adapted to small homes. To avoid disconnection between the different parts of the house, the design breaks up the continuous floor plates into multiple platforms. The section cut of the building resembles Amidakuji, or Ghost Leg, a kind of graphical lottery in which a fixed number of verticals (pillars) are connected by randomly arranged horizontal lines (floors). The living room is placed at a 6 m (20 ft) height, with views of Mt Fuji, while the remaining thirteen mini-floors sit at varying heights. The absence of partition walls results in a 'high-density domestic scenery'; privacy is ensured by placing the bedroom and bathroom above the eye level of those standing on the living or dining floors.

PARTITIONS

CLOUDS, RONAN AND ERWAN BOUROULLEC (P. 234)

TRANSFORMER APARTMENT
VLAD MISHIN

This design for a 60 m² (646 sq ft) apartment was developed by architect Vlad Mishin as a possible solution for a previous project. The inconvenient layout required optimization, which was achieved with the addition of a transformable partition wall, dividing the space and integrating a number of functions. Clad in faceted plywood, the black-metal structure splits into sections to define the apartment's different areas. A pivoting panel separates the bedroom and the living room, supporting a TV screen and bookshelves shared between the two rooms. Another section incorporates a kitchen niche, which is concealed behind a pair of folding doors when not in use.

NORTH TILES, CLOUDS

STOCKHOLM, SWEDEN
RONAN AND ERWAN BOUROULLEC / KVADRAT.DK

'Textile in architecture is something that has been forgotten in the last thirty to forty years,' says Ronan Bouroullec. 'Le Corbusier was interested in the medieval use of carpets, when people travelled with them because it was cold inside the castles, and a carpet on the wall or the floor made it warmer. We use textile for exactly the same reasons.' A collaboration with Swedish textiles manufacturer Kvadrat led to the pioneering idea of building partition walls out of textile-based tiles. His brother Erwan explains further: 'Textile has a great nomadic leitmotif, that of a yurt you roll up and take with you. For the future, we should find a way to design homes with less walls. Today there may be two of us in an apartment, tomorrow we are three or even four, then eventually we are back to being two, and sometimes we are left alone.' The use of lightweight textile walls, like the ones built with the North Tiles (above right and opposite) or Clouds (right), is an alternative to consider.

PLUG-INS & ADD-ONS

COMPOSITE HOUSE PROTOTYPE II, SU11 ARCHITECTURE & DESIGN (PP. 238–9)

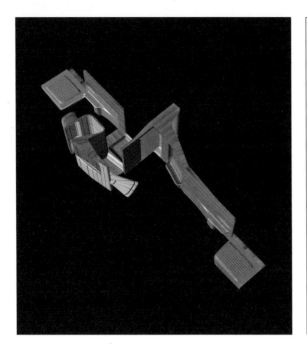

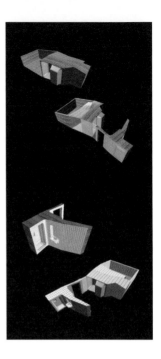

COMPOSITE HOUSE PROTOTYPE II
SU11 ARCHITECTURE & DESIGN

With this project, Ferda Kolatan and Erich Schoenenberger of su11 have reversed the conventional approach to housing design. Composite House Prototype II invites clients to configure their homes using a catalogue of functional units in a variety of materials, textures and colours. Usually, the design process 'starts with the external building envelope, then moves to interior design and finally arrives at furniture layouts,' note the architects. Here, it is the other way round: the layout of functional units determines the qualities of the living space, and ultimately the final shape of the building. The main areas of a home – living, dining, bedroom – morph into 'malleable interstitial spaces, which stretch between individual components'.

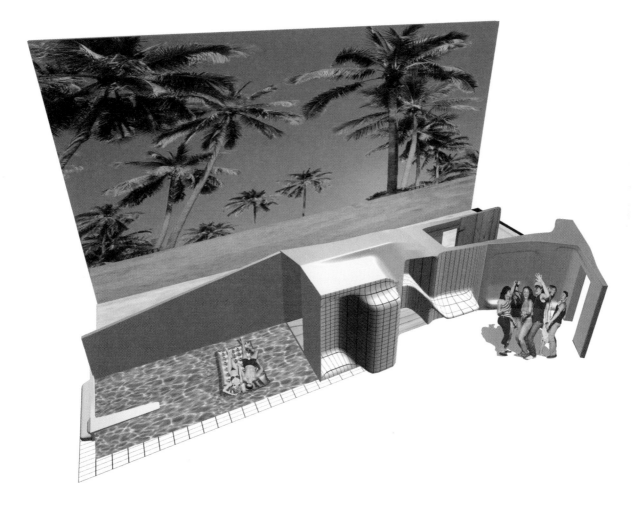

FUA MOBILE STAND
BROISSIN ARCHITECTS

Ring-shaped modules are combined to form an exhibition stand for a Mexican blinds manufacturer (left); the size and configuration of the stand can be adapted to any particular trade fair. Broissin Architects treated the space as an envelope that delineates the brand's territory, slicing it into modular fragments, and deforming some of the rings to accommodate different functions. These rings form a sculptural object-space that is cost-efficient and easy to produce and assemble.

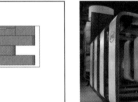

K RESIDENCE
NEW YORK, NEW YORK
SU11 ARCHITECTURE + DESIGN

This remodelled flat for a young couple (opposite) applies some of the add-on principles from the architects' Composite House Prototype II (previous pages). 'The separation between bedroom and living room had become problematic with the arrival of children,' they note, 'and the existing storage spaces were no longer adequate.' They resolved the two contradictory requirements – to open up the small apartment, while adding more storage – with the multifunctional 'Interior Sleeve'. Constructed from wood and customized Corian, it wraps around the walls and ceiling, widening and narrowing to create nooks and niches.

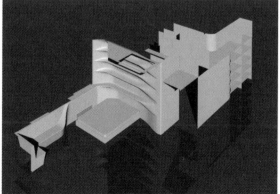

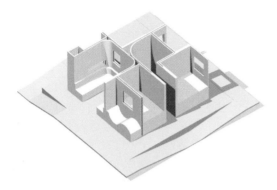

MERRY-GO-ROUND
RUINEN, NETHERLANDS
BUREAU IRA KOERS

'While the confined space of a boat or caravan has led to clever design solutions, the country cottage has never developed an identity of its own,' notes designer Ira Koers, who breaks the mould with this project for the Lanka Bungalowpark in Ruinen, Netherlands. Merry-Go-Round inverts the traditional floor plan, with rooms opening onto a central hallway. Instead, the rooms are replaced with eight alcoves, interlocked within a compact, rectangular plan and connected by a corridor that embraces the perimeter of the house.

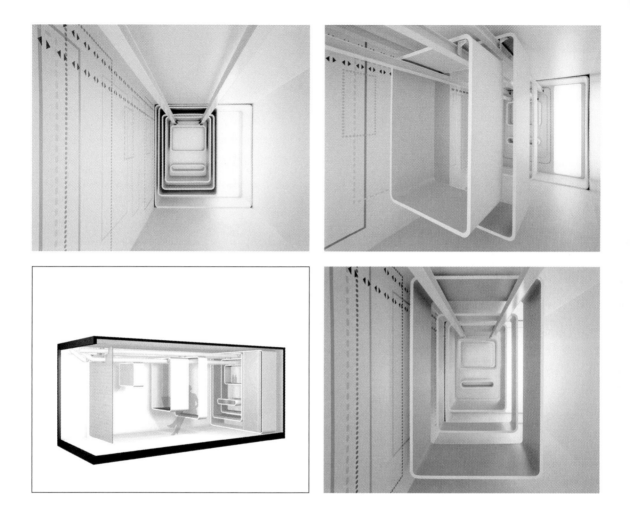

CIRCUIT BOX
STUDIO X DESIGN GROUP

In this project, Oscar Brito and Lara Rettondini of Studio X Design Group push two trends – the shrinking size of modern flats, and their increasingly flexible layout – to the limit. The design uses a series of nested 'plug-ins' to fit a variety of uses and activities into a standard container unit. The largest of these, anchored to the wall, incorporates the kitchen and bathroom and serves as a docking station for the other rings, which slide along a track rail system and are equipped with a series of user-selected accessories. A combination of several rings enables different settings, from a dining room to a study or bedroom.

BUILDING BLOCKS

CHIDORI FURNITURE,
GC PROSTHO MUSEUM RESEARCH CENTRE

AICHI PREFECTURE, JAPAN
KENGO KUMA & ASSOCIATES

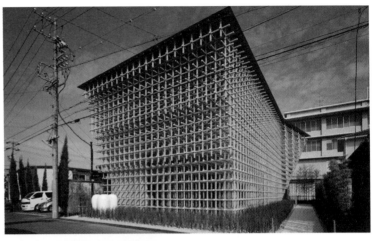

Taking a single cell and expanding it into an organism is a recurring theme in Kengo Kuma's work. The scale of the object may vary from furniture to buildings, as seen in the Chidori series (far left) for East Japan Project, and in the museum designed for the GC Prostho Museum Research Centre (above, left and opposite). Chidori, based on a traditional Japanese toy, uses a clever system of interlocking notches to build a three-dimensional lattice from square wooden sticks. It needs no adhesives or nails, and is extremely easy to dismantle. Structural tests have confirmed that the technique can be applied to architectural projects, and the entire museum was built with a Chidori-based grid, providing both structural stability and exhibition displays.

CELL BRICK HOUSE

TOKYO, JAPAN
ATELIER TEKUTO

For the design of this unique three-level house, in which steel boxes stand in for building blocks, architect Yasuhiro Yamashita of Atelier Tekuto used what he calls the 'void masonry' technique. Each box measures 90 × 45 × 30 cm (35 × 18 × 12 in.); its street-facing side is 9 mm (⅓-in.) thick, while the others have a uniform thickness of 6 mm (⅛ in.). Prefabricated units comprising five or six welded boxes were assembled on site with the help of high-tension bolts. Void masonry walls and floors do not require reinforcement, as the egg-crate structure is stiff enough to be load-bearing. The boxes also serve as storage units, distributed evenly all over the house, and provide protection from the sun. The NASA-developed ceramic coating further protects the steel structure from overheating.

GRID
PETER J. LASSEN / GRIDSYSTEM.DK

Another design by Peter J. Lassen, the champion of simplicity and functionality, this project is an organizational system, based on a single cube with an edge of 40 cm (16 in.). Here, an elementary building block is reduced to a nylon and fibreglass wireframe, fitted with a few mounting holes. Complemented by accessories that include solid sides, drawers or soft seating pads, GRID can be built up into anything from a bedroom closet to a room divider, a single-unit stool to a whole outdoor pavilion.

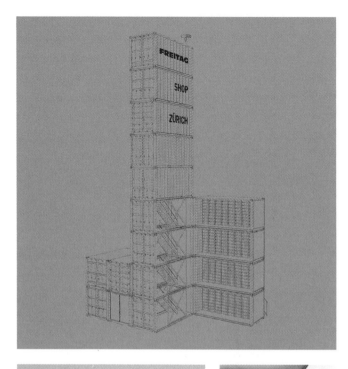

FREITAG STORE
ZURICH, SWITZERLAND
SPILLMANN ECHSLE ARCHITEKTEN

Size doesn't matter: a freight container
or a cardboard box may equally
be used as building blocks. Freitag,
a manufacturer of design bags
in recycled tarpaulin, teamed up with
architects Annette Spillmann and Harald
Echsle to stack a total of seventeen
containers into the Freitag Store (left),
'Zurich's first bonsai skyscraper'.
The tower comprises four different
stacks, including the four-container-
high retail section, fitted with Freitag's
signature display system: an assemblage
of cardboard boxes that serves as
both packaging and display.

ENDESA PAVILION
BARCELONA, SPAIN
IAAC

Endesa Pavilion (opposite), a working
prototype of self-sufficient architecture,
shaped by its immediate climatic context,
uses a construction system developed
by the Institute for Advanced
Architecture of Catalonia. The geometry
of its façade is defined by 'solar bricks':
parametric software calculates the size
and shape of each brick, depending
on orientation of the façade, seasonal
conditions, position within the wall, and
so on. As a result, the building's outer
skin mutates from active and permeable
on the southern side, to opaque
and protective to the north. The bricks
ensure energy collection, insulation
and ventilation; as they are hollow, they
also function as storage units to free up
valuable floor space.

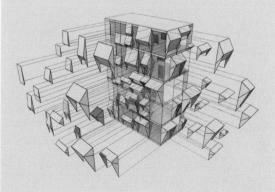

STONE CARD CASTLE,
POLYGONIUM

KENGO KUMA & ASSOCIATES

For his design for an exhibition pavilion, Stone Card Castle (right), Kengo Kuma explored the structural principle of a house of cards, using a triangular module formed by three planes to create lightweight yet robust stone constructions. Another design for display furniture, called Polygonium (below), was assembled from extruded aluminium panels with fixing joints. Despite their apparent fragility, the structures are strong enough to be used in architecture: as well as exhibition stands, Kuma also designed a residential project based on the same principle.

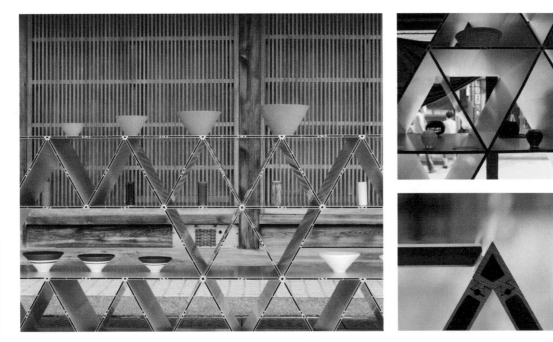

FINAL WOODEN HOUSE

KUMAMOTO, JAPAN
SOU FUJIMOTO ARCHITECTS

The design for this wooden house, described by architect Sou Fujimoto as 'ultimate wooden architecture', was conceived by stacking blocks of timber with a section of 35 cm² (5 sq in.). A highly versatile material, wood can be shaped into any building element, from beams to window frames. Fujimoto approaches this versatility from a different angle, creating an 'amorphous landscape', in which distinctions between walls, furniture, floor and ceiling are blurred, and functions are discovered, rather than prescribed. Overall, the design suggests a new, three-dimensional way of inhabiting a house.

MULTI-SCALE

100 APARTMENTS, JAKOB + MACFARLANE (PP. 258–9)

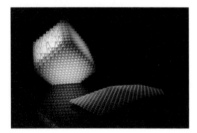

QUADROR

DROR BENSHETRIT / QUADROR.COM

Designer Dror Benshetrit's space-truss geometry, known as QuaDror, took four years to develop into a structural system that would be adaptable to a range of configurations, from tables to sound barriers, bridge pillars to affordable housing. 'Some applications take advantage of the load-bearing capabilities,' he explains, 'while others capitalize on its acoustic properties, ease of manufacture, collapsibility and energy performance.' A QuaDror module consists of four identical L-shaped pieces, which interlock to create a trestle structure or a solid panel. Possible applications include a 3D-printed luminaire for MGX (above left), modular housing units built with collapsible QuaDror frames (top right) and retail furniture for a Creative Rec showroom (middle row, centre) and Cut25 store (opposite).

FLORENCE LOEWY BOOKSTORE

PARIS, FRANCE
JAKOB + MACFARLANE

When bookstore owner Florence Loewy wished to accommodate both sales and stock within a 45 m² (484 sq ft) saleroom (right, middle and bottom), it sounded next to impossible. 'After six months of meetings, we came up with the idea of a space completely filled with books,' says Brendan MacFarlane of architectural firm Jakob + MacFarlane. 'This led to imagining a big mass of bookshelves, built using 36 × 36 × 36 cm (14 × 14 × 14 in.) modules. The idea was that inside this grid, a flâneur would walk in, pick up a book, keep on going. Moving though the grid, he «ate» out most of it with his body, leaving only three «totems». These totems became structures with bookshelves on the outside and stock inside.'

100 APARTMENTS

PARIS, FRANCE
JAKOB + MACFARLANE

A few years later, the potential of the concept developed for the Florence Loewy Bookstore was realized in a housing project (top and opposite), which was hampered by strict regulations that included the preserving of existing trees and sightlines. The team decided to test the bookstore approach at city-scale. 'We started working with the idea of a 3D matrix that our constraints could carve into,' says MacFarlane, 'and all of a sudden they changed from being problems to being something exciting.'

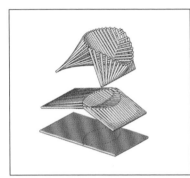

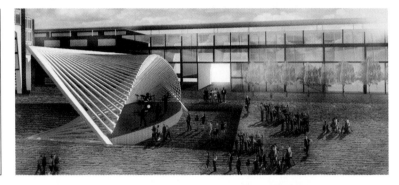

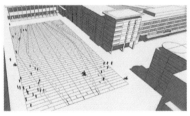

RISING CHAIR, SHIFT & MERGE, MARKET STAND

AMSTELVEEN, NETHERLANDS
ROBERT VAN EMBRICQS

Robert van Embricqs's design for the Rising Chair (top left and opposite) emerged from a few cuts in a flat surface, paired with a careful 'listening' of the material as it guided him towards the right shape. The idea of articulated beams that turn a plane into a structure was further adapted for Shift & Merge (top right and middle row), a pavilion that would serve as a shelter and covered stage or merge with the ground when not in use, as well as a system of market stands (bottom row) for the central square in the Dutch town of Amstelveen, which would fold up one by one.

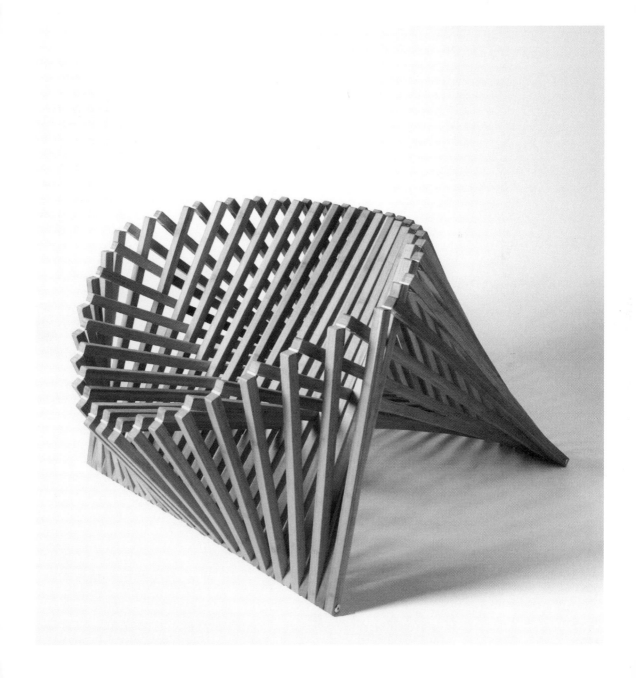

PROJECT CREDITS

606 UNIVERSAL SHELVING SYSTEM [22]
Design: Dieter Rams
Production: Vitsoe (vitsoe.com)

HEROIC SHELVES, HEROIC CARBON DESK [23]
Design: Martin Szekely (martinszekely.com)
Production (Heroic Shelves): Galerie Kreo
(galeriekreo.fr)
Production (Heroic Carbon Desk): Martin Szekely

RANDOM [24]
Design: Eva Paster and Michael Geldmacher,
Neuland Paster & Geldmacher (neuland-id.de)
Production: MDF Italia (mdfitalia.it)

SENDAI [24]
Design: Toyo Ito (toyo-ito.co.jp)
Production: Horm (horm.it)

DISPLAY SHELVES [24]
Design: Alex Macdonald (alexmacdonald.co.uk)
Production: E&Y (eandy.com)

FLAT.C [25]
Design: Antonio Citterio
(antoniocitterioandpartners.it)
Production: B&B Italia (bebitalia.com)

TIPI [26]
Design and production: Assaf Israel (joynout.com)

WEAVE [26]
Design: Chicako Ibaraki (chicakoibaraki.com)
Production: Casamania (casamania.it)

FRAMEWORKS [20–1, 27]
Design: Mieke Meijer and Roy Letterlé,
Studio Mieke Meijer (miekemeijer.nl)

SLICE [28]
Design: KiBiSi (kibisi.com)
Production: &tradition (andtradition.com)

YUU [29]
Design: Toton & Co (toton.it)
Production: YUU (yuu.eu.com)

MINIMUMBOOK [30]
Design: Giuseppe Amato
Production: MinimumBook (minimumbook.com)

SPIRAL [30]
Design: Philippe Nigro (philippenigro.com)

PARALLEL [31]
Design: Stephen Burks (readymadeprojects.com)
Production: Modus (modusfurniture.co.uk)

COMFY CARGO CHAIR [31]
Design: Stephan Schulz
(studio-stephanschulz.com)

R.I.G. [32]
Design: Mikal Harrsen
Production: MA/U Studio (maustudio.net)

GRIDLOCK [33]
Design: Philippe Malouin (philippemalouin.com)
Edition: Next Level Galerie

DRIZZLE [34]
Design: Luca Nichetto (lucanichetto.com)
Production: Gallotti & Radice (gallottiradice.it)

USEFUL LIVING [34]
Design: Sanghyeok Lee (leesanghyeok.com)

XYZ [35]
Design: Lhoas & Lhoas (lhoas-lhoas.com)
Production: Moca (mocaline.com)

ES [35]
Design: Konstantin Grcic (konstantin-grcic.com)
Production: Nils Holger Moormann
(moormann.de)

R.A.C. [66]
Design: Mikal Harrsen
Production: MA/U Studio (maustudio.net)

TERRERIA [67]
Design: Marco Casamonti, Archea Associati
(archea.it)
Production: Moroso (moroso.it)

D&V FLAGSHIP STORE [70–1]
Stockholm, Sweden
Design: Guise Architects (guise.se)

TOTEM [72]
Design: Vincent Van Duysen
(vincentvanduysen.com)
Production: Pastoe (pastoe.com)

INVADER [72]
Design: Maria Bruun (mariabruun.com)

LONDON [72]
Design: Meike Harde (meikeharde.com)

ROPERO [73]
Design: Hierve (hierve.com)
Production: H Furniture (hfurniture.co)

LAVEER, CALICO [73]
Design: Nicolas Bellavance-Lecompte and
Jakub Zak, Oeuffice (oeuffice.com)

PYRAMID, REVOLVING CABINET [74]
Design: Shiro Kuramata
Production: Cappellini (cappellini.it)

PTOLOMEO [75]
Design: Bruno Rainaldi
Production: Opinion Ciatti (opinionciatti.com)

STRATES DESK [76]
Design: Mathieu Lehanneur (mathieulehanneur.fr)
Production: Objekten (objekten.com)

AIR [76]
Design: Daniele Lago
Production: Lago (lago.it)

ETAGE [77]
Design: Claesson Koivisto Rune
(claessonkoivistorune.se)
Production: Offecct (offecct.se)

MONTANA [78]
Design: Peter J. Lassen
Production: Montana (montana.dk)

HYPERNUIT OFFICES [79]
Paris, France
Design: h2o Architectes (h2oarchitectes.com)

SUTOA, DRAWER SHELF [80]
Design: Keiji Ashizawa (keijidesign.com)
Production (Sutoa): Frama (framacph.com)
Production (Drawer Shelf): Tanseisha
(tanseisha.co.jp)

LEATHER COLLECTION [68–9, 81]
Design: Maarten De Ceulaer
(maartendeceulaer.com)
Production: Nilufar (nilufar.com)

VERO DRESSER [82]
Design: NADAAA (nadaaa.com)

STAIR.CASE [82]
Design: Danny Kuo (dannykuo.com)
Production: Opinion Ciatti (opinionciatti.com)

STACK [83]
Design: Shay Alkalay and Yael Mer, Raw Edges
(raw-edges.com)
Production: Established & Sons
(establishedandsons.com)

F009 MANHATTAN [84]
Design and production: Dick Hillen and Richard
Schipper, Founded (founded.nl)

I-JOIST [85]
Design: Steven Banken (stevenbanken.nl)

PERFORMA NUF [85]
Design: Udo Schill and Timo Küchler,
Beyonddesign (beyonddesign.org)
Production: Performa (performa-nuf.de)

INDUSTRY [86]
Design: Benjamin Hubert (benjaminhubert.co.uk)
Production: Casamania (casamania.it)

CONTAINER [86]
Design: Alain Gilles (alaingilles.com)
Production: Casamania (casamania.it)

ARTSHOP 10 [87]
Basel, Switzerland
Design: ZMIK (zmik.ch)

AESOP FILLMORE STREET [88–9]
San Francisco, California
Design: NADAAA (nadaaa.com)

FJARILL, IO [92–3]
Design: Jakob Jørgensen (jakob-jørgensen.dk)

VEGETALE [94]
Design and production: Randy Feys (rform.be)

JOY [94]
Design: Achille Castiglioni
Production: Zanotta (zanotta.it)

THE OUTSIDER / THE INSIDER [95]
Design: benandsebastian (benandsebastian.com)

DRAWER HOUSE [170–1]
Tokyo, Japan
Design: Nendo (nendo.jp)

GARY'S APARTMENT [172–3]
Hong Kong, China
Design: Gary Chang, Edge Design Institute
(edgedesign.com.hk)

NEIL BARRETT [176–7]
Tokyo, Japan
Design: Zaha Hadid Architects (zaha-hadid.com)

RICHARD CHAI [178]
New York, New York
Design: Snarkitecture (snarkitecture.com)

LUNA [179]
Design: Claesson Koivisto Rune
(claessonkoivistorune.se)
Production: Dune (dune-ny.com)

RADIO NEXT [180]
Moscow, Russia
Design: SL*Project (ab-sl.ru)

LE VIGNE [180]
New York, New York
Design: MADLAB (madlabllc.com)
Collaborators: Spurse (spurse.org)

THE WORLD'S LONGEST TABLE
FOR ALL CULTURES [181]
Design: UNStudio (unstudio.com)

CIRCLE [182]
Design: UNStudio (unstudio.com)
Production: Walter Knoll (walterknoll.de)

DUNE FORMATIONS [183]
Design: Zaha Hadid Architects (zaha-hadid.com)
Client: David Gill Galleries

OCD [184]
Design: Héctor Esrawe
Production: Esrawe (esrawe.com)

SEVENSISTERS [185]
Basel, Switzerland
Design: ZMIK (zmik.ch)

FIFTH AVENUE SHOE REPAIR [186]
Stockholm, Sweden
Design: Guise Architects (guise.se)

SPAR FLAGSHIP STORE [187]
Budapest, Hungary
Design: LAB5 (lab5.hu)

DIAMEDIA MINDS OFFICE [188]
Hasselt, Belgium
Design: Karla Menten Architecture
(karlamenten.be)

KU 64 [189]
Berlin, Germany
Design: Graft Architects (graftlab.com)

ALICE EUPHEMIA [190]
Melbourne, Australia
Design: Edwards Moore (edwardsmoore.com)

BLUEFROG MUSIC CLUB [174–5, 190–1]
Mumbai, India
Design: Chris Lee and Kapil Gupta,
Serie Architects (serie.co.uk)

DURAS DAIBA [192]
Tokyo, Japan
Design: Chikara Ohno, Sinato (sinato.jp)

SHUN*SHOKU LOUNGE [193]
Osaka, Japan
Design: Kengo Kuma & Associates (kkaa.co.jp)

SUITCASE HOUSE [202–3]
Beijing, China
Design: Gary Chang, Edge Design Institute
(edgedesign.com.hk)

TEXTILE PAVILION [204]
Luxembourg City, Luxembourg
Design: Ronan and Erwan Bouroullec
(bouroullec.com)
Client: Musée d'Art Moderne Grand-Duc Jean

RECLAIM [205]
Design: Harry Gugger (hgugger.ch); Léopold
Banchini, Bureau A (a-bureau.com)
Production: Reclaim (reclaim.bh)

WALDEN [206]
Design and production: Nils Holger Moormann
(moormann.de)

TA ĐI ÔTÔ [200–1, 207]
Hanoi, Vietnam
Design: Bureau A (a-bureau.com)

GRAPH [208]
Beijing, China
Design: Sami Rintala, Dagur Eggertsson and
Vibeke Jenssen, Rintala Eggertsson Architects
(ri-eg.com)
Client: National Art Museum of China

PENTHOUSE ON THE LOIRE [209]
Nantes, France
Design: Benjamin Avignon and Saweta Clouet,
Avignon-Clouet Architectes (avignon-clouet.com)

LOFT HAMBURG [210–11]
Hamburg, Germany
Design: Graft Architects (graftlab.com)

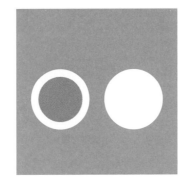

DESIGNERS

PHOTO CREDITS

All illustrations are provided courtesy of the designer, architect or manufacturer, unless otherwise noted below:

1 (middle) Lance&John; 1 (right) Inge Prins; 9 (top right) Andreas Sütterlin; 10 copyright Verner Panton Design; 13 Arch. Ignazia Favata/Studio Joe Colombo, Milan; courtesy of Studio Joe Colombo; 20–1 Raw Color; 23 Fabrice Gousset; 24 Timor Britva; 27 Raw Color; 30–1 courtesy of Philippe Nigro (drawing), VIA08 Fillioux & Fillioux; 32 Fintan Damgaard, Mikal Harrsen; 33 Alexandra B; 34 (top middle, bottom middle and right) David Stjernholm; 35 (bottom, left and right) Jäger & Jäger; 36, 37 (left) Max Rommel; 38 Nicolas Genta; 39 Daisuke Shimokawa / Nacása & Partners; 40–1 NakaniMamasaxlisi Photo Lab; 43 Daisuke Shimokawa / Nacása & Partners, Inc; 45 (left, top and bottom) Rudi Schroeder; 46 (bottom) Chanan Strauss; 47 (bottom) Mette Bersang; 48 courtesy of the artist and Herald St, London; 50 Sara Anfossi (stools); Alexander Mahmoud (details); 51 NakaniMamasaxlisi Photo Lab; 52 Paolo Contratti; 54–5 Max Rommel; 56 (top, left and right) Bona-Lemercier Architectes; 56 (bottom), 57 Florian Kleinefenn; 58 (left, top and bottom) Jäger & Jäger; 62 (top) Fillioux & Fillioux; 65 Max Rommel; 66 Fintan Damgaard, Mikal Harrsen; 67 (right) Alessandro Paderni; 67 (bottom left) Pietro Savorelli; 68–9 Nilufar Gallery; 71 Brendan Austin; 73 (bottom left) Nicola Tree; 76 Julien Renault; 79 Julien Attard; 80 (bottom left) Mizono Daichi; 80 (right and top left) Kenpo; 81 (left, top and bottom) Nico Neefs; 81 (right) Nilufar Gallery; 82 Dan Bibb; 83 (left) Mike Golgwater; 88–9 Juliana Sohn / courtesy of Aesop; 90–1 courtesy of Yohji Yamamoto; 95 Stamers Kontor; 97 Oliver Wrobel / Bianca Elmer; 98 (top left) Studio SKLIM; 98 (top middle and right, bottom) Jeremy San; 99 courtesy of Yohji Yamamoto; 105 Luca Campigotto; 107 Adam Mörk; 114–15 Fien Muller; 116 (top left) Alberto Parise; 116 (top right) Santi Caleca; 116 (bottom) Kristof Vrancken; 117 (left, top and bottom) Sadamu Saito; 117 (right) Pim Top; 119 Jeremy Eichenbaum; 129 (bottom) Jeppe Gudmundsen-Holmgreen; 130–1 Inge Prins; 132 Miquel Merce Arquitecte; 133 Hiroshi Mizusaki; 136 Álvaro Benítez; 137 Norihisa Ishi; 138 Rasmus Norlander; 139 Daici Ano; 140 David Grandorge; 141 Jesper Lindstrøm; 142–3 Akihiro Ito; 144 Jasper Reyes, Kamil Krol; 145 (top) Roel van Tour, Pim Top and Mathijs Labadie; 145 (bottom) Paul Tahon, Ronan and Erwan Bouroullec; 146–7 Hiroyuki Hirai; 148 (left) Akihiro Ito; 149 Filippo Bamberghi; 150 (bottom), 151 Sadamu Saito; 152 Simon Bouisson; 154 Randy Cockran; 155 Nicolas Guiraud, Cats Factory; 156–7 Louis Baquiast / courtesy of Aesop; 158–9 Gidon Levin; 161 Miquel Merce Arquitecte; 162 Daici Ano; 163 Louis Baquiast / courtesy of Aesop; 164 (drawing) SMH+U, (photos) Paul Warhol; 165 Philippe van Gelooven; 166 Frank Oudeman; 167 Julien Attard; 168–9 Katherine Lu; 170–1 Nacasa & Partners; 174–5 Fram Petit; 178 (top, left and right) Snarkitecture; 178 (bottom) David Smith; 181 (bottom left) Roland Borgmann; 183 (top) ORCH; 183 (bottom) David Gill Galleries; 184 Juan Navarro; 185 Tom Bisig; 186 Lance&John; 187 Zsolt Batár; 188 Philippe van Gelooven; 189 Tobias Hein; 190 Tony Gorsevski; 191 Fram Petit; 192 Takumi Ota; 200–1 Boris Zuliani; 204 Paul Tahon, Ronan and Erwan Bouroullec; 205 Christian Richters; 206 Jäger & Jäger; 207 Boris Zuliani; 208 Pasi Aalto; 209 Thierry Malty; 210–11 Tobias Hein; 212–13 Shen Zhonghai; 214 Pasi Aalto; 216 Daria Scagliola; 217 Jeroen Musch; 218 Stéphane Chalmeau; 220–1 Paul Ott; 225 Hiroyasu Sakaguchi; 226–7 Hervé Abbadie; 229 Daici Ano; 230–1, 234–5 Paul Tahon, Ronan and Erwan Bouroullec; 241 Ty Cole; 243 Daito Masami; 244–5 Iwan Bann; 246 (top right and middle right), 247 Daici Ano; 248 Makoto Yoshida; 250 Roland Tännler; 251 Adrià Goula; 253 Iwan Baan; 254–5 Paul Rafferty; 257 Nathan Kraxberger; 258 (top) James Ewing; 259 Nicolas Borel

To Rem, sensei and complice

Furnitecture: Furniture That Transforms Space © 2015 Anna Yudina

Designed by Anna Yudina

First published in 2015 in hardcover in the United States of America by
Thames & Hudson Inc., 500 Fifth Avenue, New York, New York 10110

thamesandhudsonusa.com

Library of Congress Catalog Card Number 2014944629

ISBN 978-0-500-51776-5

Printed and bound in China by Everbest Printing Co Ltd

STACKED OBJECTS
EMIEL REMMELTS

Citing the avant-garde Russian artist El Lissitzky as an influence,
Emiel Remmelts designs items of furniture (below and on
p. 2) that only remain standing thanks to an eclectic mix of
construction materials and found objects, which complete the
'unfinished' wooden structures.